CASE STUDIES IN

CULTURAL ANTHROPOLOGY

GENERAL EDITORS

George and Louise Spindler

STANFORD UNIVERSITY

HENNAGE

A Social System in Miniature

HENNAGE

A Social System in Miniature

By

CLEMENT HARRIS

HOLT, RINEHART AND WINSTON, INC.

NEW YORK   CHICAGO   SAN FRANCISCO   ATLANTA

DALLAS   MONTREAL   TORONTO   LONDON   SYDNEY

Library of Congress Cataloging in Publication Data
Harris, Clement, 1938–
    Hennage: a social system in miniature.

    (Case studies in cultural anthropology)
    Bibliography: p. 95
    1. Great Britain—Rural conditions—Case studies.
I. Title. II. Series.
HN385.5.H29   309.1'426   74–2352
ISBN 0–03–005756–6

Foreword

About the Series

These case studies in cultural anthropology are designed to bring to students, in beginning and intermediate courses in the social sciences, insights into the richness and complexity of human life as it is lived in different ways and in different places. They are written by men and women who have lived in the societies they write about and who are professionally trained as observers and interpreters of human behavior. The authors are also teachers, and in writing their books they have kept the students who will read them foremost in their minds. It is our belief that when an understanding of ways of life very different from one's own is gained, abstractions and generalizations about social structure, cultural values, subsistence techniques, and the other universal categories of human social behavior become meaningful.

About the Author

Clement Harris is a pseudonym. The author was born in London, educated at Eton College, and worked for some years at the British School of Archeology in Jerusalem. On his return to England he became fascinated by the social structure of the villages of East Anglia where he had lived for some time. This led to his going up to Magdalene College, University of Cambridge, to read* social anthropology. He took his degree, B.A. (Honours), in social anthropology, which enabled him to return to the Middle East, the area of his major professional interest. He is at present attached to a university in Norway and is engaged in fieldwork among the Rwala Bedouin. His main interest is in nomadic peoples, with a strong preference for the Arab world. He is married to an anthropologist and has three children, all of whom, at the moment of this writing, are living with him in his Bedouin tent.

About the Book

This is a study of a small community in East Anglia, a part of England and yet separate from it in certain ways, both geographically and culturally, that will be as strange to most American readers as many tribal communities in remote lands. The author describes Hennage after long and intimate contact with the community. And yet he must describe it, in one sense, as an outsider, for membership in the "core group" of "real Hennage people" is limited to only a few of the village residents, and according to certain criteria that the author is able to make clear. A picture emerges of a closed community, though not quite closed,

* This is customary usage for study in a particular field in England.

for over time new members are added to the core group and, of course, people leave it by death and migration. The "real Hennage people" are caught up within, and maintain by their behavior a social system in miniature. This social system deals with the outside world and with the powers that are perceived as present in the environment, so that the system may survive. The system also deals with its own members, particularly those who might or do deviate from its norms, and it provides its own system-sustaining myths, some of which the author describes in the process of creation.

In Hennage the difference between the inside and the outside of the system is great. The "us" and the "them" distinctions are the very substance of the system. It is this insulated distinctiveness that many people, uprooted from their home communities by migration or urbanization, are nostalgic about. Yet this in itself is one of the reasons why people migrate from the cozy ingroup of the small community to the at least initial anonymity of the city. One's roles, in fact one's self, are ascribed by the system and its monitors. The only escape is death or migration. These factors have doubtless played a role in migration from small communities to urban centers in England and elsewhere for generations.

Mr. Harris writes as an Englishman, with the idioms of English in the land of its origin. Since English, spoken or written in this manner, is partly a foreign language to most Americans, words and phrases that could be unfamiliar to the American reader are explained either in the text or in footnotes.

This case study is of interest for several reasons. It is the only study so far in this series about an English village or community of any sort, and as the author explains in the last chapter, it is not really paralleled by any other existing study of a community in England published to this date. It is the result of intimate familiarity with the ins and outs of life in a very small group, and the author has been able to combine an anecdotal, at times almost gossipy, style of reporting with an analytic stance and models derived from social anthropology.

GEORGE AND LOUISE SPINDLER
General Editors

Stanford, California

Preface

This study is concerned with a small village in Norfolk, a part of the region referred to as East Anglia, whose last king was defeated in A.D. 870 by the Danes. Since then it has always been part of a larger political unit without ever losing its identity as a region. Indeed, the rest of England is still contemptuously referred to as "the Shires" (pronounced "Sheers"). East Anglia was of major importance during the Middle Ages as a primary wool-producing area. This trade subsequently declined until the land is now almost exclusively arable; the tradition of shepherding has only recently died out in Hennage and still continues nearby. It is an area of large estates, intensively farmed by some of the most highly mechanized farmers in the world. The crops are mostly barley, sugar beets, and vegetables. The climate is relatively dry, with 25 to 35 inches of rain a year, mostly in the winter but otherwise well scattered throughout the year. (England as a whole can scarcely be said to have a "dry season.") The temperature varies from an average of about 60 to 65 degrees F during summer to 30 to 35 degrees F during winter, though it fluctuates considerably. There is usually at least a breeze and often high winds off the sea to the north and east. In winter they are very cold indeed, especially those from the north, which sweep down from the Arctic with no mountains to impede their passage.

Communications with the rest of England are, by modern standards, poor. Stuck out into the North Sea, the region has never been a through route to anywhere. Even now communications with the Midlands are pathetic. There is no direct train service and the roads are totally unable to cope with the volume of traffic. The best roads (and trains) lead to London, although it was pointed out with a certain pride in the local paper that Norfolk, the fourth largest county in England, still, in 1970, had no motorways and only eleven miles of dual carriageway. There are no physical obstacles to the building of larger roads ("very flat, Norfolk"), but the population is one of the least dense in England, though in recent years it has been increasing faster than any area of comparable size. The increase has been, and still is, due to immigration rather than a higher birth rate, and more "new towns" are planned to take the overspill from the great conurbations. This development seems to have increased regional consciousness. Not only is the regional Anglia television watched almost to the exclusion of all other channels but the local accent seems to be reasserting itself. In Hennage the younger villagers speak with a much more pronounced Norfolk accent than do their parents, and for many years, until the death of the author, the "Bor John" dialect letters in the Eastern Daily Press were one of its most popular features. This popularity is not confined to the working class. "Bor John" letters in book form are found in many upper-class houses, and the best-known exponent of

Norfolk dialect is himself upper middle class. He was recently elected "Norfolk-man of the Year" by an overwhelming majority of Anglia television viewers. It should be pointed out that he did not "learn" the dialect; it is a natural medium of expression, although he speaks Oxford English as well. In this he is not alone; many of the gentry switch from one mode to the other depending upon their audience. If there is any condescension, it is directed toward outsiders. Thus the gentry, largely indigenous, as are many of the landowners, present a cultural homogeneity. This concept of themselves as inhabiting an area unlike the rest of England was well summed up by William Hastings, the local dairyman, who once asked a guest of mine, "Well, what do you think of this funny old place?" With the large-scale immigration to the new towns, as well as numerous holiday-makers and weekenders, the consciousness seems to become more acute.

This consciousness is not only on an East Anglian scale; people from King's Lynn, West Norfolk, coastal North Norfolk, North Norfolk, East Norfolk, Norwich, the Broads, and South Norfolk are also distinguished by accent, though it takes an acute ear to catch the difference, and there may be other criteria as well. Each area seems to regard itself as "true Norfolk," but all unite in a common front against other regions of England. It is against this social and economic background that *Hennage* is set.

A word of warning—I have used the phrases and words "core group," "villager," and "village" in an apparently inconsistent manner. This is not wholly so. Where the distinction is important and relevant I have always used core group; where it is unimportant, that is, where more than the core group is meant, I have used villager or the village, depending on common English usage. It should be clear from the context exactly about whom I am writing.

CLEMENT HARRIS

Acknowledgments

I am indebted to many people for this study: first to my supervisors at Cambridge for their continual encouragement and valuable suggestions and to the staff at the Social Anthropological Institute at Bergen University for their interest and constructive criticism. Although many suggestions from these sources have been incorporated, all criticism should be directed at me; I am solely responsible, while any success should reflect the quality of their teaching; I have simply tried to apply it. The debt due my wife is enormous. Not only did she encourage me, but was ruthless in her disapproval of passages which did not come up to the standards she was trained to at London. I am also grateful to the Vicar for allowing me ready access to the registers and other documents in his charge. Finally, to all the people of Hennage I must remain extremely grateful. I cannot thank them all by name; to do so would not only be invidious but would destroy the *noms de guerre* I have used to protect their privacy. Their names have been changed throughout, as have the names of all but large towns, but I have attempted to preserve the flavor of the originals. If some of them appear improbable, it is because they are, to our eyes, improbable in reality; I have actually invented none.

Map 1. England showing East Anglia.

Map 2. *East Anglia showing counties and relevant towns in Norfolk.*

Contents

HENNAGE

A Social System in Miniature

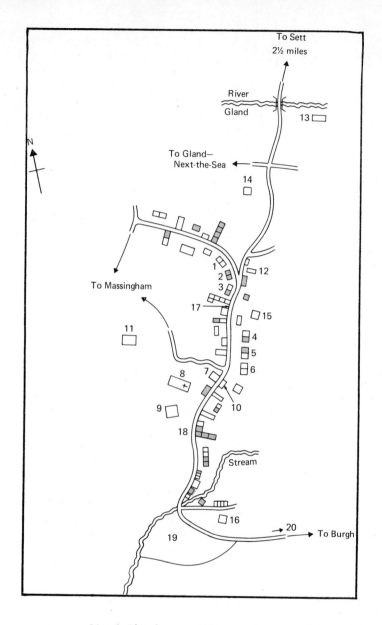

Map 3. Sketch map of Hennage (not to scale).

1–6.	Council houses	14.	Hill Farm
7.	Shop	15.	Town Farm
8.	Church	16.	White House Farm
9.	Vicarage	17.	Foundry gates
10.	Baptist Chapel	18.	Nightingale's nest
11.	Hall Farm	19.	Common
12.	Garage	20.	To Dairy with school one
13.	Mill Farm		mile further on

Shaded buildings indicate houses inhabited by core-group members.

Introduction

PHYSICAL SETTING

Hennage is a small village surrounded by largely arable, gently rolling farmland. The fields are large, divided by hedges, and the pattern is broken up by "plantations" (copses) for the pheasants, for this is great shooting country. Hennage follows the road from Sett, which eventually reaches Thetford, for some half-mile, with only one offshoot of about a hundred yards along a minor road toward the next village north. It is relatively compact; the only major open area was filled by the council houses[1] in 1946. Apart from the council houses the cottages are of flint and brick with red pantile roofs. There was a public house, but it is now closed. There is one shop/post-office, combined now with an off-license,[2] a flourishing garage cum agricultural contracting business, and an undistinguished church. There are four outlying houses: Hill House, formerly a farm and now a middle-class residence; two other farmhouses, one formerly the Mill; and the Hall, also a farmhouse. All these farms are inhabited by tenant farmers and have been for the last seventy years. The land surrounding the village is good but not top-quality agricultural land, almost exclusively under cultivation, though earlier more livestock was kept, notably sheep. A few water meadows at the southwestern end of the village are grazed by store cattle[3] from Hall Farm, and a small dairy herd is kept at Town Farm at the other end of the village. The surrounding parishes are all agricultural with the exceptions of Sett, two-and-a-half miles to the northeast, and Burgh, two-and-a-half miles in the opposite direction. Burgh had the only heavy industry in the area, but there is now some light industry in Sett, which was formerly the market town; nowadays the works at Burgh are converted to light industry. The physical isolation of Hennage is not extreme, but the bus service is poor and there is a sense of isolation not wholly borne out by the ease of local communication.

The houses which make up the village are not apparently better or worse than most nearby villages. By modern standards, their chief defects are that they are mostly too small and too old. Their size is chiefly a function of the material used

[1] Council houses: Houses owned and managed by the local council.
[2] Off-license: A shop where alcoholic liquor for consumption off the premises may be bought.
[3] Store cattle: Bullocks and barren cows which are fattened and then killed for beef.

1

The Hall.

for building. It is impossible to span large spaces when the walls are of spherical flints unless those walls are extremely thick, for the old lime mortar used was not strong enough on its own to counteract the outward thrust of the roof. This applies particularly to the older cottages, but later cottages built of brick are not much bigger, and any enlargement must be by building on or by converting two cottages into one, a fairly frequent practice in recent years. As is common in North Norfolk, the stairs are appallingly steep—indeed, so steep that a broomstick placed upright from the newel post makes a splendid hand rail with the stairs twisting round it. Apart from the council houses, only three cottages have been built this century. These conform more closely to Parker-Morris[4] standards, but diverge strongly on matters of plumbing and drainage. Electricity came in the 1930s, mains water in 1962. Mains sewage is not contemplated in the forseeable future. On the arrival of mains water the council houses were given inside standpipes, and most of the cottages had at least a standpipe[5] near the back door. Before 1962 only four houses had water closets, but since then more have been installed, notably in the council houses, which were fully plumbed in 1971, the drains running to septic tanks. Before the introduction of the mains, water was collected from a variety of wells scattered up and down the village or from pumps outside the back doors of groups of cottages, with the exception of a few larger houses which had private boreholes[6] with electric pumps to a roof tank.

[4] Parker-Morris standards: Minimum standards for new houses laid down by Parliament following the recommendations of the Parker-Morris Committee.

[5] Standpipe: A tap connected to the mains water but outside the house, usually by the back door.

[6] Boreholes: Pipes driven down to tap underground water, which is drawn up by suction; not a well.

Cottage; note ironwork.

In size the cottages vary from small to very small, the latter being one up and one down, the former two up and two down. Although an estate agent might find difficulty in describing them in glowing terms, except in those of visual attraction, they are definitely not rural slums, although they could degenerate into such if it were not for the care taken of them by their inhabitants. The only building of any architectural distinction is the Hall, formerly the summer residence of the Bishops of Thetford. This is the fourth outlying house, though perhaps isolated would be a better description as it is only a hundred yards from the shop and the church.

HISTORICAL BACKGROUND

Hennage is first mentioned in the Domesday Book,[7] the etymology of the name being Old English, and the only points of interest are that the manor was held by the Bishops of Thetford, and that in common with all East Anglia, it had a very high proportion of freemen. At the dissolution of the monasteries[8] the manor was given to Henry VIII's physician, whose descendants held it until it was sold to the present owner's family, the Lords Stamford, in 1710. In the eighteenth-century directories it is simply mentioned as a village on the road from Thetford to Sett. It is described more adequately in the nineteenth-century directories, for they give lists of gentry, tradesmen, and craftsmen. Even so, it is one of the

[7] Domesday Book: A compilation of land use and population ordered by William I (1066–1087) and completed in the next reign.

[8] Dissolution of the monasteries: When Henry VIII was made supreme head of the Church of England in 1534, monastic institutions were closed and their property sold off to the highest bidders.

shorter entries. By this date Lord Stamford owned three quarters of the parish, and by the end of the nineteenth century he owned all the land except for two fields—under 1 percent of the total acreage. It must be made clear, however, that Hennage is not in any sense an "estate village." Lord Stamford owns neither the cottages nor the land on which they are built, merely the agricultural land. The cottages are owned either by their occupiers or by small capitalists, mostly local tradesmen and tenant farmers, not necessarily belonging to the village, who built or bought the cottages as an investment against retirement.

The greatest change was the building of the railway in 1884. That the railway came to Burgh at all was an accident. The chosen spot was two miles further south at Wood Norton, but that village was still in the throes of enclosure.[9] The railway balked at the probable delay and was offered Burgh instead by Lord Stamford. Burgh was near enough to provide jobs but far enough away not to impinge socially. It is odd that the grain for export continued to go six miles to the coast to be shipped from Gland-next-the-sea rather than the two miles to the railway in Burgh. It was not until the coming of the railway to Sett, in the 1890s, that the grain went by rail at all. It is unclear why grain carts should go up the steep hill to Sett and not along the relative flat to Burgh, but all local memories are of the great wagons breasting the rise to Sett. Burgh was not only a junction but a railway works, and many men gained skills there which were readily transferable to mechanized agriculture and its service industries when the works closed in 1936. The two world wars left the village relatively unscathed, as both agricultural and railway work were reserved[10] occupations. The increasing mechanization of agriculture after World War II has been partially offset by the growth of service industries in the immediate neighborhood. Finally, it should be noted that Hennage is the only village in the parish. It is at the most northern edge of Lord Stamford's Norfolk estates and at the western edge of the Rural District Council in which it is a constituent part.

THE MODEL

To make the subsequent analysis more readily comprehensible let us construct a model of Hennage and its social system. On a national level Hennage shares its language, political system, and economic environment with the rest of the country; it is part of Norfolk, which is part of East Anglia, which is part of England, and so on. Within the agricultural system possible patterns can be viewed thus:

A. Type of Landholding
   a. Landowning
   b. Land renting
   c. Landless

B. Type of Farming
   a. Pastoral
   b. Arable
   c. Horticultural
   d. Mixed

[9] Enclosure: The enclosing of land held on the old open field system or of common wasteland by acts of Parliament from the sixteenth to the nineteenth centuries.

[10] Reserved: During both world wars workers in certain occupations were exempt from military service.

Hennage falls squarely into AcBb, though all other types occur in East Anglia in all possible combinations in patterns of great diversity. Thus for Hennage the only relationship possible between villagers and landowners is one of employee-employer. Whatever the variations possible within the type of landowning (and they could range from national company, private estate, to independent farmers large or small), none of the owners need have any tie with the village except in their capacity as employers. In Hennage, as it happens, there is one absentee landlord who owns virtually all the land, renting it out to three or four tenant farmers. It is important to note that the relationship maintained between landlord and tenant, in this instance, is asymmetrical, being that of superior-subordinate. It must be made clear that there is no attempt to build up a lord-client relationship with its mutual obligations, for no tenancy has ever been heritable. Indeed, it is deliberate policy that no son should be allowed to follow his father on a tenant farm. This of course means that tenant farmers are concerned with immediate profit rather than with farming "for their grandchildren." There is very little "feel for the land" in Hennage. Similarly, the only relationship between the tenant farmers and the villagers is again asymmetric, one of superior-subordinate, employer-employee. It is with the lives of the villagers, the base of the hierarchy, that this study is concerned.

On the political side, the power structure runs from the County Council to the Rural District Council to the Parish Council. However, this is a relatively new system, the traditional structure having run from the Lord Lieutenant of the County to the gentry to the villagers. Only the latter part of this hierarchy concerns us here. The gentry were of great importance, because it was only through the control of land that any direct access further up could be achieved. The linkage between gentry and villagers could be through the intermediaries of tenant farmers or the Vicar, himself a member of the gentry by virtue of his position. In Hennage both these intermediaries played their parts. To return to the modern power structure, it is relevant to note that in Hennage, as in many other villages, the Vicar is the *de facto* chairman of the Parish Council, and the only prominent long-term member is the tenant farmer at the Hall, as it always has been.

Similarly in the field of education, power runs from the county education authorities to the boards of governors of the schools. The chairman of the board of governors of the the local school is the Vicar, and the board members are tenant farmers and other members of the middle classes.

The third great institution, law, is more difficult to assimilate to this model. In earlier times the Parish Constable was responsible to the Parochial Church Council; later he was replaced by the village policeman, who was responsible to the county police authorities headed by the Chief Constable. (Since 1969 we have had no policeman in Hennage.) The other side of the law, the courts, are at this level magistrates courts, and while the position of Magistrate is open to all, it is still the domain of the relatively affluent. It is perhaps convenient to subsume the big landowners, the Chief Constable, Magistrates, etc., under the heading of the "Establishment"—and to a large extent the Establishment hold the power. The one area where that power in its traditional guise is weakened is in the organization of local government. The total power structure then is twofold: the traditional, leading directly to the Establishment, and the new, leading to the County Council.

Land agent inspecting the crops.

The mediators between the landless laborers and the upper echelons of the power structure may vary widely. In an urban situation trades unions are obvious candidates. However, in our rural area the unions are weak; the farmers, the Vicar, shopkeepers, and small entrepreneurs (taking over the position of the crafts-men, the traditional radicals) could fill this role. But in Hennage all possible media-tors in a village structural role lead back indirectly to the landlord. The landlord

Retired farm worker.

owns the land which the farmers use; he appoints the Vicar, he owns the shop, and estate work is the mainstay of the entrepreneurs. It is axiomatic, then, that only those directly dependent on the landlord, at the apex, can fill the structural role of mediator between apex and base. Other individual members of the middle classes who simply happen to live in the village are not part of the system and thus can have no structural position. The traditional mediators who filled these roles continue to do so, for the Vicar and the tenant farmers are members of the Parish Council. Nobody in Hennage appears to know the representative on the Rural District Council for Hennage (it is the tenant farmer at the Hall), so the Parish Council cannot be circumvented in this way. By both structures, then, the land-owner, Lord Stamford, has power over the villagers, although there is no evidence that he ever used it. It is interesting that the attitude of the villagers remains traditional, with Lord Stamford subsumed under an all-pervading "Them," which is institutionally opposed to the villagers' view of themselves as "Us." The only attempt ever made to circumvent him and "Them" through manipulation of the Parish Council was initiated by the Agricultural Workers Union, which virtually collapsed in 1926.

For Hennage, then, a simplified model appears thus:

Economic	*Political*
Landowner	County Council
Tenant farmers and Vicar	Parish Council (Tenant farmers and Vicar)
Villagers	Villagers

This simple model has, of course, changed somewhat in recent years. Not all the villagers are so closely connected with farm work as in the past; many of them work in small building firms, garages, a dairy, joineries, and so on, which have direct access to the outside world. Yet many of these small firms, notably the builders and the dairy, are still directly dependent on the landowner, for it is estate work or the herds of tenant farmers which supply their bread and butter. The "old-boy" network in an area of large estates is still enormously powerful and has ramifications in the County Council as well as within the traditional estab-lishment structure. This is not to suggest that the "old-boy" network is actively used for political or economic machinations, but the villagers are aware that it exists. Their attitudes toward the outside world are still molded by the assumption that not only does the old social order continue—as in part it does—but that it is still operative. The relevance of this statement will become apparent when I ex-amine the norms to which the villagers adhere. The norms are dominated by a desire to remain inconspicuous together with a strict sense of egalitarianism. In a hierarchical system where power goes from top to bottom, the motto at the bottom seems to be "Out of sight, out of mind."

METHODOLOGY

Hennage was chosen as the subject of this study for no scientific reason; I happen to have a house there, chosen for personal reasons, and from the start I simply wished to understand how the village worked as a social system. One factor which helped was that my mother-in-law was Welsh. Until she moved to Hennage I had missed much of the significance of village behavior. Being of East Anglian stock myself, in many instances I regarded as normal behavior that my mother-in-law saw as curious, and I took for granted customs that she as an outsider found unpalatable. Actually, being resident in the village has had advantages and disadvantages. The main benefit was that I was a normal part of everyday life. As my family come from North Norfolk, I was never regarded as a total outsider. Also, all my children were born in the village. These factors eased my contact with the villagers considerably, a contact which, according to many accounts, is exceedingly difficult to obtain. The main disadvantage is that I have had to be extremely circumspect, for I have to go on living in the village. This has not affected my conclusions, but I have had to circle endlessly round a topic until the information has come out spontaneously or not at all. The use of the direct question has had to be minimal.

The collection of information fell into four phases. The earliest was one of orientation, when I was largely motivated by my own curiosity and I collected material haphazardly with no thought of publication. Next was a phase of inquiry into attitudes toward education, conducted in two other villages as well. This was carried out by means of questionnaires coupled with interviews by my wife or myself. While this method performed a useful function, it became clear that it had severe limitations in areas that aroused people's emotions. In the third stage I wanted to quantify the degree of geographical mobility on the part of the villagers, which seemed to be high. This meant compiling a complete list of inhabitants from 1885 onward, and it was accomplished mostly by research into the written records. As a piece of research it was not a great success, partly because of inadequate records and partly because of the difficulty of delimiting the field. But it did mean that I now had at my disposal an almost complete genealogical record of every villager, together with details of when and where each had moved. By the time the final stage of straight anthropological fieldwork came, I was on very good terms with the rest of the village. They were used to me and were ready to tolerate my visits to them with hours of chatting—though, in fact, these sessions were fairly carefully structured. The majority of people were very patient and accepted my questioning as an interest in local history, an eminently suitable and topical occupation for one such as myself. A minority were patient in the extreme. They realized that I was after more than local history and were enormously helpful, often answering personal questions directly and frankly. All this has taken some eight years and has involved participant observation, questionnaires, interviews, extended case studies, and one piece of social engineering. All were useful in their way, though the questionnaires were of very limited value owing to the prevailing attitude of giving the answer that would get the questioner out of the house fastest. The same objection to formal interviews was apparent except for carefully selected individuals. The piece of social engineering I attempted was a fête.[11] From my point of view the express purpose was to identify village leaders, and this aspect of it was a total failure. However, the negative result initiated a new approach to the

[11] Fête: A common English entertainment for the purpose of raising money for a church, school, or charity. Usually a fete takes place in the garden of the local big house. Traditionally, there are stalls of homemade goods, competitions and raffles, simple games of skill, teas, and an entertainment such as country dancing. Often known as the "fete worse than death" by the organizers and sometimes the participants.

analysis which proved fruitful. As a fete it was enormously successful—a fact which certainly enhanced my reputation, and organizing it at all certified me as a normal middle-class member of the village.

My use of statistics is minimal, mostly because of the small size of the sample at my disposal. With the population of Hennage fluctuating around one hundred to one hundred and ten adults, the employment of statistical methods seemed a waste of time; with this quantity every case is a special case and the final figures for inclusion become meaningless. Further, the demographic composition of the village is odd and I was uncertain how this would affect the results. When my first child was born he was one of three children under eleven years old in the entire parish, and one of only twelve under twenty-one (six of whom were siblings). As a result of family movements there are now over twenty children of eight and under and only one teenager among the villagers. The next group up are in their middle to late twenties, mostly the parents of the aforementioned children. Above them there is a gap to their parents' generation, or to be more accurate, to other adults of their parents' age. The rest of the villagers are elderly. For some time this demographic imbalance worried me, but I noticed that other villages had oddly weighted populations too, and I began to suspect that there is an oscillation of age ranges between various villages which add up to a normal distribution.

1 / The core group

Hennage at this particular time has some one hundred and ten adult inhabitants, of whom about ninety would be classed as villagers, the rest middle class. It is from the broad category of villagers that the core group is drawn. The definitive indication I had that such a group exists was when I organized the fête. This was a deliberate piece of social engineering on my part, although it was designed to raise money for a popular village project. I had previously been aware that the villagers regarded themselves as a community, or at least some of the villagers did, but I could find no trace of any leaders. I was more naive in those days, and although fully aware of acephalous[1] societies, I assumed that a subsystem within a total hierarchical society should itself be hierarchical. My original plan was to fade into the background as soon as the organization of the fete got underway to allow the "natural leaders" to come to the fore. However, this became impossible because of the total inability of any person to make any decision at all on his own or others' behalf. With hindsight I can see why, but at the time it puzzled me. Several people had experience of fetes and gave freely of their time, reminiscences, and advice, but none would suggest or do anything on his own. At meetings someone might say to nobody in particular, "Ooh, wouldn't it be nice to have a dance then?" There would be a hum of approval and many recollections of other dances, ending with, "We always used to have a dance in the old days; you ought to ask Mrs. So-and-so, she'll tell you." However, nobody would ever admit to having made the original suggestion or willingly take part in organizing it unless pressed. This happened for every single event and stall which we subsequently had. But like a theme, several names came up over and over again of people whom I was advised to consult. These people never came forward voluntarily, indeed, none of them ever came to a meeting, but it was clear that they were the people to whom the villagers looked for guidance. This seemed to be the mechanism whereby any suggestions or ideas could be franked with the mark of "village approval": they themselves could then partake with a clear conscience; they hadn't gone beyond their "place." I didn't recognize this as leadership at first, but it is a clear example of leadership from behind. It maintains the fiction of egalitarianism while providing guidance and authority within the group. Having gained this approval, everybody cooperated fully and worked very hard to make the fête the success it was.

[1] Acephalous societies: Societies with no formal leadership. See J. Middleton and F. Tait, *Tribes without Rulers* (London: Routledge & Kegan Paul, 1958).

It was the corporate nature of the group that prevented the villagers from suggesting or organizing a fete on their own. I had suggested the fete as a means of getting money for play equipment for the children on the common[2]—a situation which members of the core group had been grumbling about. This was acceptable to the group, but how the fete was to be organized was up to me, and ideas I had of which they did not approve were ignored. This was clearly demonstrated by the fate of the flower and vegetable show I organized, on the dogmatic grounds that village fetes ought to have them. The response was unenthusiastic, and later, elaborately evasive. Not a single member of the core group entered a flower or vegetable. Only a few incomers, most noticeably the gamekeeper, participated, and my show was an unmitigated disaster. I should have realized that the villagers, with their strong sense of egalitarianism, would avoid occasions of competition. Nobody wanted competitions such as baby contests or sports at the fête. The only exception was a tractor-driving contest, but this was in fun rather than in earnest. The only really competitive element that was allowed to creep in was Hennage against the other villages, and the winner's pleasure stemmed from the fact that he had shown the superiority of Hennage over Massingham and elsewhere. Indeed, the winner gave his prize money back to the fête.

After the fete I asked every person in the village to mark on a complete list of villagers the names of those whom they considered to be "real Hennage people." The middle-class informants and very recent arrivals in the village returned lists that were completely individual responses, depending largely on geographical location within the village. The replies of longer-resident villagers fell into two categories. The core group (the "real Hennage people") marked only each other, while the others produced varied responses which, on the whole, agreed fairly closely with the core group's definition of "real Hennage people." The discrepancies mostly reflected age differences—the young tended to include all those older than themselves, while the old included all their contemporaries while leaving out the young. Apart from this their lists agreed very closely, and the core-group lists did not show the age discrepancies. Young incomers' lists seemed to reflect length of residence rather than genealogical connection, but for the most part all the lists delimited with fair accuracy a group of people generally recognized as the core of the village. Henceforth I shall refer to these persons as the core group. No middle-class person was ever included on the lists, either by himself or by others. The people whom I had been advised to consult about the fête were all core-group members. From the genealogical information I had already collected it became apparent that all "real Hennage people" were connected in some way. Except for very close relations, relationship was always in terms of "some sort of a cousin," and this phrase also included those who were only connected by marriage. As I had complete genealogical records of the families concerned from the parish registers, I could see the exact relationship, and it became clear that kinship among "real Hennage people" was of bilateral kindreds of rarely more than three genera-

---

[2] Common: A piece of land of variable size held "in common" by the village for the village in perpetuity. Originally for the gathering of firewood, grazing of animals, and so on, the common is now more usually used for recreational purposes. These uses are guaranteed by law.

tions' depth. All members of the core group are linked by marriage at least, even though many of these links are in the forgotten past and have been incorporated under common cousinship.

To be a "real Hennage person" obviously meant something. People were described as "a Sett woman" or "a Massingham man," as if the adjective was loaded with meaning. Only rarely was anyone said "to come from" somewhere, and then the individual concerned was either an incomer or from a village outside the normal range of the system. Almost no one who was a potential core-group member was described as "coming from Sett," but was always referred to as "a Sett person." This variation of description is interesting, as it indicates the villages that have a similar social system, enabling the individual or family to slip neatly into place. Having constructed the genealogies, it was possible to check each person's position in relation to someone else with a similar genealogy and life history. When a distinct difference in status between two people with similar genealogies and life histories except for one or two factors appeared, it was possible to ascribe the difference in status to that factor. If the pattern was repeated with other people, it became clear that it was indeed that factor which produced the variation. Widowhood is an obvious example and has the added advantage that the change can be observed on the death of the spouse. Childlessness is another, and I had the satisfaction of seeing the theory fulfilled when a young couple had their first child after several years of marriage. Their status changed from merely potential core-group members to actual core-group members, albeit well down the scale because of their youth. By similar checking of factors the ideal villager emerged. Of course, nobody measured up to it, though a few came quite close, and it became apparent that there were other factors which I had not taken into account. These factors were behavioral and were measured by how closely the participants adhered to the village ethos.[3] This theory proved much more difficult to ascertain, as it entailed a preliminary investigation of village norms.

Some years earlier I had investigated the attitude toward education in Hennage and two other villages. This had given me an insight into the alien nature of the social system I was investigating. If a society in Africa or New Guinea is being analyzed, the alien nature of that society is assumed. But in England one does not expect to find a subsystem that wishes to operate as a closed system. For example, education was regarded as irrelevant to their lives; it was imposed on them from above and was submitted to with bad grace. Young illiterates with whom I have talked were proud of their achievement in passing through the entire educational system untouched. At the time I was unable to account for this attitude, but merely accepted it as a fact. Using hindsight, it becomes clear that educational success attacks the strong village norm of egalitarianism. This is illustrated in the story of Dennis Williams, which he told to me spontaneously. He came from a nearby village with his family, but despite its nearness it clearly belong to another type of system. On arrival in Hennage Williams immediately aroused resentment by occupying one of the coveted council houses. He set out to overcome this

---

[3] Ethos: Norms and values; the abstract of ethical behavior.

resentment by playing a full part, as he thought, in village affairs. To this end he organized cricket matches, whist drives, joined the Parish Council, and "represented" the village to the Vicar. Accordingly, he was shunned and thoroughly disliked by the core group. Realizing what had happened, Williams dropped all his activities and, quite literally, cultivated his garden. After a long period he gradually became accepted by the core group, though, of course, he did not become a core-group member. He was quite explicit as to the reasons for their dislike and the factors which led to his subsequent redemption. He had gone beyond his "place," notably in the matter of "representing" the core group, and had drawn attention to himself in a manner completely unacceptable to that group. He had, in short, contravened the egalitarian norm which forms the basis of village behavior.

GENEALOGIES

It became quite clear when full genealogies were drawn up that the vast majority of those whom I had tentatively designated as potential core-group members were related in some way or another to either the Dobson, Clare, Clare-Hoveringham, or Hoveringham families. Length of genealogy was unimportant. Both the Dobsons and the Clares had been in the village for only three generations, while the Hoveringham family, who now have little role in the core group, have been in Hennage in the direct male line for at least six generations and possibly from the sixteenth century. I will start with the Dobson family, as they illustrate most clearly how a family expands and consolidates its position as a core-group family. For ease of reference I shall provide a shortened family tree including only those who still live in the village (Figure 1.1).

Old Harold Dobson married Talitha Neal in 1881. The Neals are referred to as "real Hennage people." Though they have since died out in the male line, they were numerous at the beginning of the present century. James Harold married Bessie Victoria Durrant, another "real Hennage family," the last male of which died a few years back. Their offspring include Hannah, Joan, and

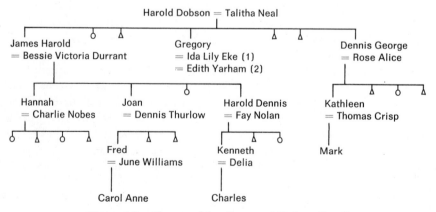

Figure 1.1—Shortened family tree of Dobson family.

young Harold. Hannah is not very intelligent and was married off to Charlie Nobes, who came to Hennage as an orphan from Pulham Market workhouse to work as an under gardener at the vicarage. Their children no longer live in the village. Joan married Dennis Thurlow, a "Wood Norton man," and had, among others who have left, Fred, who married June Williams; they have a daughter, Carol Anne, and live in the village. Young Harold married Fay Nolan from Sett—she is described as "coming from Sett, her mother was a Sett woman," a nice distinction which neatly sums up her position in the village, as will be shown later. Their children include Kenneth, who is now married to Delia, "a Sett woman"; they have an infant son. Returning to the second generation, we find that Gregory married twice, both times endogamously within the village, which is rare. His first marriage was to Ida Lily Eke, by whom he had a daughter who now lives outside the village; his second marriage, after his first wife's death, was to Edith Yarham. The Yarhams were "real Hennage people," so prolific, intermarried, and uninventive about Christian names that, as none remain in the village, I have been unable to disentangle their family tree. By this marriage, too, Gregory had a daughter who married a "Stewkey man" and who still comes over to look after her widower father. Gregory's brother Dennis married Rose Alice and had, among others since left, Kathleen, who married Thomas Crisp from Basham—the same village, incidentally, from which old Harold had originally come. Whether Thomas Crisp is a descendant of Aurora and Savory Crisp of Hennage I am unable to say, but there is certainly a close link between the villages, which is odd considering their distance apart. Kathleen and Thomas Crisp have a young son Mark and live in the village. Of the people mentioned, the following are still alive and resident in the village: Gregory Dobson, Dennis Dobson, Hannah Nobes, Joan and Dennis Thurlow, Fay, Kenneth, Delia, and Charles, Harold, Kathleen, Thomas, and Mark Crisp, and Fred, June, and Carol Anne Thurlow.

The next family to be considered is the Clare family. I shall give a short version of the family tree for simplicity (Figure 1.2). From being a well-entrenched

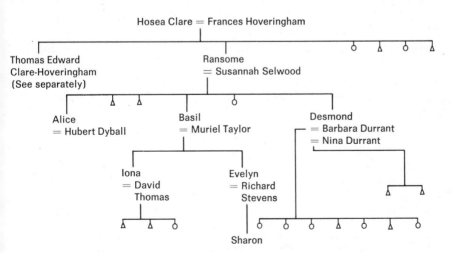

Figure 1.2—Shortened family tree of Clare family.

Hennage family the Clares have gone into dissolution and now only three of them remain. Hosea Clare arrived from Derby, it is said, in the 1850s and married Frances Hoveringham, a member of the only really long-term Hennage family. Of their several children only two concern us—Thomas Edward, who was born three years before they were married, and whom I shall consider as a separate family, and Ransome. Ransome married Susannah Selwood, "a Burgh woman," and had Alice, Basil, and Desmond, among others. Alice married Hubert Dyball, a member of a family which has for some generations moved constantly between Hennage and Little Hennage in the next parish. They are childless. Basil married Muriel Taylor, from a Sett family of publicans, and had two daughters, Iona and Evelyn. Iona married a man from Burgh and later moved to Peterborough; Evelyn married Richard Stevens, a "dealer's son" from Sett, though they are now separated. Both daughters have children. Desmond "married" twice, two sisters, one legally and in church and the other in common law;[4] they shared the same house and worked as one family. The two sisters, Barbara and Nina Durrant, are nieces of the Bessie Victoria Durrant who married James Dobson. Between them he has had nine children and has recently moved to Burgh, though he was still resident in Hennage for most of this inquiry. Nina, who was never officially married to Desmond, was "married off," to use the local expression, to a Londoner, after bearing Desmond Clare two children who continue to live with him. For the purposes of this study, the following still live in the village: Alice and Hubert Dyball, Muriel Clare, Evelyn, Richard, and Sharon Stevens, and Desmond, Nina, and Barbara Clare. The rest have died.

The next family to concern us is technically part of the Clare family—Thomas Edward Clare-Hoveringham and his descendants. Why his parents waited three years after his birth before marrying is unclear, as is his choice of surname. It is not the usual practice to take a double name for children born out of wedlock, and, in fact, he has been variously registered as Clare, Hoveringham, Clare-Hoveringham, and Hoveringham-Clare. This matter of names has been a constant source of confusion in compiling these and other genealogies. Names are not constant in this area. For example, Mears becomes Mayes; Clare was originally Clear; Hubert George Dyball was registered as George Herbert Diball; Barbara Durrant is really called Amy (her cousin really is called Barbara). These inconsistencies, coupled with an uninventiveness about Christian names (in some families, though not in all, as may be gathered from a survey of some of the names used in Hennage), resulting in the use of nicknames, has made the compiling of genealogies a complex business. It was this factor, as well as the affinal nature of being "a real Hennage person," which concealed in the beginning the interrelationship of the core group; at first glance the choice of members is arbitrary.

To return to the Clare-Hoveringhams as they are now known (Figure 1.3): Thomas Edward I married Elizabeth Briton and had many children, among them Thomas Edward II, Maud, and Alfred. Thomas Edward II married

---

[4] Common law: Sanctioned by neither church nor state, the living together of a man and woman is regarded for many purposes—for example, inheritance—as a legal marriage.

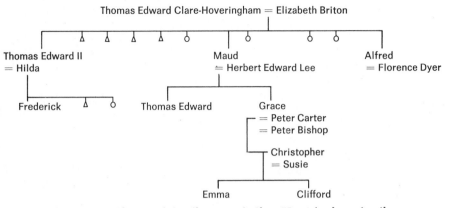

Figure 1.3—Shortened family tree of Clare-Hoveringham family.

Hilda and had three children, of whom only Fred, who is unmarried, remains in the village. Maud married Herbert Edward Lee, the illegitimate son of a farmer's daughter by a "traveling man," as gypsies are called here—at least that is the story. Maud and Herbert had three children—Pearl, who died as a small child, Thomas Edward, who never married and lives with his Uncle Alfred and cousin Fred, and Grace, who married Peter Carter after having had a child, Christopher, by him first. This household of Thomas, Alfred, and Fred are the only small-holders, but they do not appear to hold agriculture in very high esteem. Thomas, who keeps pigs, seems to have little affection for them. After Peter Carter was killed Grace married Peter Bishop and had a son by him. This child has since left the village. Christopher Carter, or Bishop, as he is now known, married Susie, "a Gunton girl," and on his parents' death moved into their cottage, where he now lives with his two young children. The third remaining child of Thomas Edward I, Alfred, married Florence Dyer of Sett. They live, childless, in the village with Fred and Thomas Edward Lee. Thus, the surviving members in Hennage are Alfred and Florence Clare-Hoveringham, Fred Clare-Hoveringham, Thomas Edward Lee, and Christopher, Susie, Emma, and Cliff Bishop.

The fourth and last family for which it is necessary to have details is the Hoveringham family (Figure 1.4). This family is among the earliest to appear in the first parish register in the 1560s. They have many ramifications in the surrounding villages, although these are frequently denied as cousins of any sort, though with some groups a little work on the relevant registers shows that they must be. For our purposes it is not necessary to go back further than Esau I who was born in 1832. Esau and his wife Mary Anne had three children who are relevant to this study—Mary, Esau II, and Elizabeth. Mary married a shepherd, Thomas Church, and had several children. Harold, the only one remaining in the village, married Annie and had Thomas and Alice. Thomas married a land girl[5] from London during the war and has no children. His sister Alice

---

[5] Land girl: A member of the Women's Royal Land Army Corps, formed during World War II to release men from agricultural work for the armed forces.

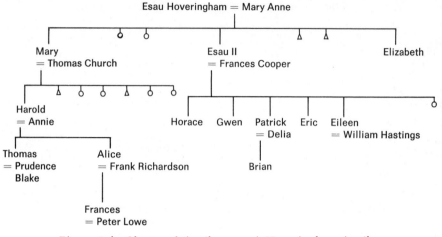

Figure 1.4—Shortened family tree of Hoveringham family.

married Frank Richardson, also a Londoner posted to Norfolk during the war. They have one daughter, Frances, who married Peter Lowe, "a Sett man." The Lowes have a baby. Esau II married Frances Cooper, one of whose sisters is reputed to be Herbert Edward Lee's mother, although I can find no trace of it in the registers. Three of their children, Horace, Gwen, and Eric, are unmarried and live together in the village. Patrick married Delia, from Southend, and they have a son, Brian. Eileen married William Hastings, the local dairyman. One of their sons, Thomas Cooper Hastings, married Avril Williams, sister of June Williams, who married Fred Thurlow. The last member of the family to be considered is Elizabeth. She is still alive, aged ninety-eight at the time of writing, living in an old people's home, and is included only because it was her husband's sister Susannah who married Ransome Clare. She is visited by her husband's sister's children, Alice Dyball, for example, but not by her own nephews and nieces. Those still remaining in Hennage are Harold and Annie Church, Thomas and Prue Church, Alice and Frank Richardson, Frances and Peter Lowe, Horace Hoveringham, Gwen Hoveringham, Eric Hoveringham, and Delia and Brian Hoveringham.

GROUNDS FOR INCLUSION

The surviving members of these four families are all related in some way or another, often through marriages with Durrants, but more important, they all conceive of themselves as being related. Both Alice Dyball, who has a remarkable knowledge of her family's ramifications, and old Thomas Church have told me, independently, that "all the Dobsons, Clares, and Hoveringhams are some sort of a cousin." The same has been echoed by others who could not trace the actual connection at all. All of these surviving members form what I call the potential core group. I had noticed that most of them formed some sort of a group, but until I worked through the genealogies I was not aware of the relationship between them. There are a few other members of the potential core group, but I will comment on them when considering other factors. The vast majority of the potential core group, then, are connected genealogically. But what makes one person an effective member and another an ineffective one?

The answer is contained in one word—"competence." To be "competent" in the village context carries a host of implications and is a portmanteau[6] word covering a whole ideal of life. Before considering who is and who is not competent, let us trace the meaning of competence and its implications. To begin with, a detailed list of factors such as age, marital status, marriage partner, number and history of children, length of residence, status of parents, and the like, was compiled. By comparing the observed status of members of the potential core group, an ideal "Hennage person" emerged. Although the ideal person, or family, does not exist, several people come fairly close to it, and it is this approximation to the ideal that I call competence. The word "competence" implies a mixture of ascribed and achieved status, but in no way implies superiority. Being incompetent need not necessarily be the individual's own fault for much rests on fate and outside occurrences. If it is accepted that the primary unit is the ongoing family of parents and children, it can clearly be seen that childlessness or early widowhood is, in some way, incompetent, through no fault of the individual.

It is important to realize that no blame attaches to the unfortunate individual; the slight moral overtone to the word "competence" is misleading, and I use the term only because I cannot find a better. It is difficult to convey the exact flavor of the concept. There is a vague feeling that fate ought to be controlled and that it is slightly incompetent not to be able to control it. Those whose fate is favorable are given credit for controlling it; those whose fate is unfavorable must in some way be incompetent. This is reinforced by the complete absence of the concept of "luck"; I have never heard this word used except in a Bingo context. This paradoxical view that fate is beyond one's control yet must be controllable, because some people appear to be more fortunate (in village terms) than others, is most clearly seen in the attitudes to suicide. The person who commits suicide is a hero. By taking his fate into his own hands he demonstrates that fate is controllable. He shows his supreme competence by denying fate. It is in this sense that competence must be understood, and for the rest of this book I shall use the words "competence" and "competent" in this way. It must be remembered, however, that competence in this sense is applicable only within the village norms of conduct. Where an individual transgresses a norm, I shall mention it as an instance of incompetence, since the abnormal is in itself incompetent.

LIFE HISTORIES

Who then on this list of potential core-group members are competent? And on what grounds are the others incompetent? I shall consider men and women separately, since the men are far less concerned with village social life.

---

6 Portmanteau: Originally a large hold-all—in this context a word containing a whole concept.

Only the elderly were prepared to be photographed: to be photographed is to be conspicuous.

I shall start with Joan Thurlow (see Dobson family tree, Figure 1), as she is, in some ways, the *doyenne*[7] of village life. She has lived in Hennage nearly all her life and has a married son living in the village. Her husband is a retired carpenter and is now mostly to be seen tending his garden. She is an efficient housewife and a good manager, intelligent and thoroughly normal in every respect, epitomizing the successfull village woman. However, her lack of more positive qualities is very important and will be apparent when I consider leadership.

Her sister, Hannah Nobes, is very different. Not quite mentally defective and with a speech impediment that makes her quack like a duck when talking,

---

[7] *Doyenne*: French word meaning the acknowledged arbiter in social matters. The epitome of social nuance; for example, if she serves tea on an embroidered tablecloth, others feel they must follow suit—an Emily Post figure.

Hannah is competent to the limit of her capabilities. Married to Bertie Nobes after having had an illegitimate child (in itself no stigma), they had a daughter who is married and has left the village, a child who died, and a son who lives in a residential home. These instances of incompetence are sufficient to ensure that she remains only a potential core-group member; but in addition she has taken to religion. For Hannah Nobes to go to church would be abnormal enough, but she goes to chapel, and an Evangelical Baptist chapel at that. (The chapel belongs to "The Society for the Evangelizing of Britain's Villages.") The Baptist chapel is new, or at least it was virtually defunct until the arrival of Sister Beattie Lamb from the Ealing Mission in London. She arrived with the express intention of evangelizing and was disliked from the start. Her subsequent domination over Mrs. Nobes has caused epithets ranging from "wicked old woman" to "cantankerous old bitch," mostly with reference to her taking Mrs. Nobes away from her husband and family. To become so dominated is an example of Hannah's incompetence, and though it is regarded as stemming from her feeble-mindedness, this does not exonerate her. Nor is there any reflection on her family for allowing her to become so dominated. Her fate was in her own hands and she could not cope; it is as simple as that. If Joan Thurlow epitomizes village success, Hannah Nobes is her opposite. Now widowed and with no children living in the village, she is demonstrably not mistress of her own fate. In other words, she is incompetent.

Fay Dobson is in a somewhat similar position. The fact that she is not a "real Hennage person" by birth is largely immaterial, since this quality is transferable by marriage. Her trouble stemmed from her husband's behavior. Although he was a "real Hennage person" by birth, he did not conform to Hennage standards, being very disagreeable and notoriously light-fingered. He died prematurely in his early fifties. Apart from these two examples of incompetence, Mrs. Dobson transgresses village norms by the nature of her work, which is at the laundry in Sett. Though working is not abnormal for village women, it is abnormal to work alone. The fact that Mrs. Dobson works with many other women is immaterial—no other *village* women work at the laundry: they either do domestic work or work together at the dairy or in gangs, carrot-picking, currant-picking, and doing other seasonal agricultural activities. No one blames her for this transgression. Indeed, it is recognized by all that Mrs. Dobson needs regular work; nonetheless the choice of job reflects incompetence, for she has gone outside the village norms. Her daughter-in-law Delia is only recently married and has a small baby; she appears to conform to village standards of efficiency and management and is on the road to core-group membership. She is as yet without influence because of her age and because she has not had a chance to display her competence; only time can do that.

Kathleen Crisp is in a somewhat similar position, though further along the same road. A managing woman with no sign of incompetence as yet, she is also "a real Hennage person" in her own right. June Thurlow is a particularly interesting case; she is a "real Hennage person" by marriage only and overcame the heavy disadvantage of her father's behavior (which was discussed earlier) to become the obvious heiress to her mother-in-law's position. She is undoubtedly competent in both senses of the word and is happily married with a daughter of fourteen. As seems to be the case with full core-group members, there is little to say about her except that she fulfills village norms and expectations.

The next family for consideration is the Clare family (see Figure 1.2). Alice Dyball is the oldest member of the family and while no longer an active member of the core group, was a key figure in the recent past. Her position lapsed when her brother Basil died and her other brother Desmond moved away, leaving her the sole representative of that generation. She is highly competent in the normal, everyday sense of the word and is incompetent in village terms only because she is childless and has an incompetent husband. This incompetence is partially overcome in two ways. First, she has a remarkable knowledge of village genealogies, which enables her to demonstrate the continuity of her family on a larger than usual scale; she is well aware of the Hoveringham connection and the Durrant connection and plays them for all they are worth. Second, she is very intelligent, with an acid, if not venomous, tongue. Thus by widening her familial horizons and by sheer personality she has mitigated her prime disadvantage. However, subsequent events in the Clare family have seriously undermined her position, and she is not nearly so influential as she once was. She is, I think, regarded as a core-group member far more by the older generation than by the younger villagers, who do not remember her so clearly in her family context, which has now radically altered.

Muriel Clare is a striking example of the social death that results from widowhood, though other factors are also involved. Fully eligible for coregroup membership through her marriage, she seems never to have been fully accepted by the others—due partly to her family background and partly to her incompetence in household matters. The first serious doubts about the Clare family seem to have been raised when Iona, the elder daughter, gained a place as a pupil at the grammar school.[8] She was the first village child to do so, and by enjoying it and accepting the middle-class norms of the place, she was cut off to a large extent from village society. This reflected on Muriel Clare's competence as a mother, and her behavior in her younger daughter's trouble confirmed it. At the age of fourteen Evelyn became the leading figure in a lurid scandal of the sort that is loved by the *News of the World*.[9] In the words of my first informant, "Every man in the village had been through her," and while this is undoubtedly an exaggeration, a number of men had been involved. This episode left little stigma on Evelyn; indeed, her mother was blamed for her behavior, for it reflected deeply on her competence as a mother. Mrs. Clare compounded her offense when she called in

[8] Grammar school: The English state education system at that date; from 5–11 years a child attended primary school; at 11 years all children took an examination and intelligence test, commonly called the 11 +, to determine which sort of secondary school they would attend. The main division was between the grammar schools, which took the "academically inclined" children, and the secondary modern schools, which provided a more practical education. This system has now changed.

[9] *News of the World*: A Sunday tabloid of a sensational nature.

the police after Evelyn had been out all night. To call in outside help is to attack the moral and emotional self-sufficiency of the group. This virtually destroyed her status in the village, and her husband's early death a few years later precipitated a social decline of startling rapidity. Now her only acquaintances in the village are Hannah Nobes, since her widowhood, and an elderly housebound recent widow who cannot get rid of her. By all others she is, as far as possible, avoided. Iona confirmed the villagers' suspicions by marrying an ambitious young railwayman from Burgh and moving to Peterborough. Evelyn has had a more varied history. Nobody held the peccadilloes of her youth against her; she married a "dealer's son" ("dealing," covering scrapdealing, entrepreneur activities, and a multitude of similar jobs, is not respectable in Hennage) from Sett and had a daughter. Despite this somewhat unfortunate marriage, she seemed in a good position to become a member of the younger core group, being very competent in the house and friendly with June Thurlow and others. But she left her husband when he brought a girl friend home to live with them and went, not home to her mother, but to live with a married man in Burgh whose wife then left him. It is just possible that this would have been accepted, but at the same time she abandoned her daughter, thus attacking a fundamental tenet of the village ideal—the continuance of the group through children of the group and their upbringing in the norms of the group. That this was the reason for her fall from grace in the village sense seems to be confirmed by an earlier instance of a similar kind concerning the late Maud Lee, but I will deal with this and point out the similarities when considering the Clare-Hoveringham family.

Barbara and Nina I am not certain about; they were never much in evidence in the village and were quite clearly dominated by their husband. I suspect that dominance by one spouse to the extent of taking a second partner is a demonstration of the incompetence of the other spouse, but as they have left the village, I cannot confirm my suspicions.

The next family is the Clare-Hoveringham family (see Figure 1.3). The only surviving females are Florence, Alfred's wife, and Susie Bishop. The household of Alfred, Florence, Fred, and Thomas Edward Lee keep themselves very much to themselves. Florence very rarely leaves the house. Her husband does the shopping, and I have never seen her talking to anyone in the village. This may be fortuitous, as they live at the far end of the village, outside my immediate range. Susie Bishop, a pleasant, capable young woman with two well-turned-out children, is liked by all and is one of the younger core-group members including June Williams and Delia Dobson.

The more interesting female members have recently died. The first was Maud Lee, Thomas Edward's mother, who ended her days as an eccentric, avoided by all. This probably stems from an episode that occurred nearly fifty years ago when Thomas was four. It was winter and he had pneumonia, but despite this he was taken out and treated as if he was simply being tiresome. His uncle and aunt, Alfred and Florence, intervened and were told they could have him if they wanted him, and he has remained with them ever since. The parallels with Evelyn Stevens' behavior toward her daughter are obvious, and the results for Maud Lee lasted until her death a year ago.

Maud's daughter Grace was a key core-group figure until her death. An indefatigable gossip, though never malicious, Grace Bishop was the main channel through which village opinion was formed and sanctions applied, partly because she delivered the papers, a job that took her the whole morning. Even after her death she remains a respected figure, perhaps largely because of her long fight against some sort of cancer. Her husband predeceased her by a week, just as she was said to have been improving. Village opinion was that he worked himself to death caring for her, and this statement may well have some truth in it for he refused to let her be taken to hospital. This mutual devotion and the fact that she simply gave up her recovery after his death was interpreted in much the same way as suicide; they had cheated fate and chosen the manner of their death. Much of the respect they earned has devolved onto their son and daughter-in-law, Christopher and Susie.

The last family is the Hoveringham family (see Figure 1.4). Annie is the oldest woman and plays little part in village affairs. Like most of the elderly women, she rarely leaves her cottage. In most cases this practice cannot be explained by physical infirmity, and I cannot account for this social phenomenon. It is as if the old abdicate in favor of the next generation, but whether this is the cause or the effect of the neglect of the old, which seems widespread in East Anglia, I am unable to ascertain. Whatever the reason, old women are rarely seen, occasionally scurrying down to the shop and exchanging words in passing but never stopping for a chat.

Prue Blake has several counts against her. First she is childless and second, she is not a good housekeeper; both represent incompetence. She also transgressed one of the important village norms. When she arrived from London during the war she worked as a landgirl; this was anomolous enough but perhaps justifiable, owing to circumstances. However, she became "wunnerful with the cows" and was in great demand by local farmers. This went right against prevailing custom, for though the harvesting of crops has always included women to some extent, the management of animals has always been a strictly male preserve. By being "wunnerful with cows" Prue Blake destroyed a firmly held myth and she has never been forgiven. Even now, if her name comes up in conversation, this is always dragged in somehow. It is said she virtually proposed to her husband, whom she visibly dominates, and whatever may be the actual situation in Hennage, the man must at least appear to be the dominant partner.

Alice, her sister-in-law, is an equally dominating woman, but disguises this more effectively and her husband is less spineless than her brother and far nicer. She is highly competent in both meanings, living in a spotless and frequently redecorated cottage and having a married daughter in the village. She is a professional seamstress, working at home, and since the decline of Alice Dyball is second only to Joan Thurlow in influence.

Her daughter Frances lives in the village and shows clearly the effect of motherhood on a woman's social position. In the early years of her marriage, Frances worked as a hairdresser in Sett. As in other places, this is one of the highest aspirations of village girls and is socially approved. In the village Frances' status was potentially high, but the actuality did not come about until the birth of the child. She is now very much one of the younger core group and is very influential within her age group, which influence will undoubtedly increase with the years, all things being equal.

Gwen is genealogically in the strongest position of all, but the incompetence of spinsterhood has effectively neutralized it. In earlier years she may have overcome this handicap, but now she is without influence and is of an extremely retiring disposition—it was some years before I even saw her.

Delia is a widow, which as we have seen is a heavy burden, but she was never a core-group member, the main reason being her feelings of superiority and her ambitions for her child. Quite apart from this, she is a devout chapel-goer, and not being able to manage without the crutch of religion seems to be regarded as incompetent, and her resignation on her husband's death—"the Lord giveth and the Lord taketh away" were her actual words—did not show a proper understanding of the malleability of fate. She is now ignored by all, save Hannah Nobes and Beattie Lamb, her co-religionists.

It is impossible to deal with the men in as much detail as the women because they are not so easily observed, being at work most of the day: but it is clear that the same criterion of competence applies to them. However, their competence is reflected in their job and garden and car as well as in the wider application of marriage and fatherhood. There are gradations of status among them, and the same types of criteria apply. As with the women, old age in itself is no guarantee of influence. Gregory and Dennis Dobson do not have much status outside the circle of retired men and as widowers not as much as old Thomas Church, whose wife is still alive. As all these men are retired and their wives are either dead or housebound, they are not in a position to take a major part in village social life.

It appears that the influential man of the core group is one who works with two or three other village men and whose wife has a strong position in the core group. Gossip and opinions are relayed to the wife in the evening and disseminated by her the following day. As the men only gossip at home, it is not easy to observe them in this activity, and consequently I may be underestimating the influence of the men. It is not of great importance to my main argument, since the status of both husband and wife interact and affect one another. It is difficult to be high in the core group if one's husband or wife is not also so regarded, although it is not impossible. Alice Dyball, for example, overcame several disadvanatges, including a weak husband, by sheer force of personality. Unable to keep a job because of chronic asthma, and regarded by the village as a malingerer, her husband has always been an ineffectual and incompetent man and has undoubtedly helped to prevent his wife from remaining a powerful member of the core group. Conversely, a high-status husband can transmit his influence to his wife if she is competent within her own domain. The obvious example of such a case is Fred and June Thurlow. His obvious competence as a carpenter and gardener, as well as his status by birth, enabled June to neutralize the effect of her father's behavior, and when her father mended his ways, take her place as a full core-group member of the younger generation. Similarly Kenneth Dobson seems to be enabling Delia to move in the same direction. This is not invariably so, as Desmond Clare's wives, though of high genealogical status themselves, never played a very prominent part in village affairs even though Desmond himself did and had as high a place as any man in the core group.

Transfers of status seem to work equally well the other way though Dennis Thurlow is the only suitable recipient in the village at the moment. None of the other marrying-in men are competent enough in their own sphere to allow it. The males of the Clare-Hoveringham family are all childless or bachelors, and all work on the land, which is an anomalous occupation at the moment. The only exception is Christopher Bishop, who has transmitted his status to his wife.

Finally, of the Hoveringham men, Harold Church, the oldest, is now too old to be influential in the core group, but he is very much respected, both for his competence as a skilled metal worker and as a core-group member. Thomas Church is a wholly ineffectual character, totally under the thumb of his wife. His influence is nonexistent, and when he is mentioned at all he is cast as a stock comic figure. His brother-in-law Frank Richardson is also overshadowed by his wife and is not very competent, changing jobs frequently. His son-in-law Peter Lowe is an unknown quantity, only recently a father. He is a skilled electrician and a careful gardener, so he will probably acquire the high social status that his wife is gaining, but it is too early to say. Horace and Eric are both bachelors, which effectively precludes much influence, and Brian, the only potential start of a new line of Hoveringhams, is unmarried as yet.

The members of these four families cover the vast majority of core-group members, but there are a few others who must be accounted for. Mrs. Euston is an elderly widow, "a Ryburgh woman" who married Thomas John Euston, who died just after Christmas in 1970. The Eustons are an old Hennage family, appearing as Useton in the 1830s. Thomas John was much respected as a skilled turner and blacksmith who worked on the railways most of his life. They only had one daughter, who lives in Ryburgh nearby and is married to a policeman. The factors that have kept Mrs. Euston as a potential rather than an active core-group member are all minor, but there are many of them. To begin with, she is somewhat superior. A highly intelligent woman, she adapted easily to life as a lady's maid to an eminent K.C.'s[10] wife in London and picked up many upper-class attitudes and interests. Although this took place many years ago it is still very prominent in her conversation and this is taken by the village if not as a desertion of village norms, at least as evidence of the desire. Her daughter's marriage to a policeman, an essentially antivillage figure, did not help, nor did her daughter's devotion to the church; not that she is a keen churchwoman but simply a keen and highly competent organist, the recreation in itself being unusual in Hennage, at least nowadays. Perhaps Mrs. Euston is best summed up as somewhat unorthodox rather than incompetent; and this unorthodoxy has not been counterbalanced, as it might have been, by a constellation of orthodox relations, for the Euston family has always been small, with rarely more than two siblings per generation.

[10] K.C.: King's Counsel—legal term, a senior barrister.

Mrs. Beryl Ives and her husband Edward are easier to account for. Her parents are Scots and came to Hennage just after the war. They fitted well into village life without ever being fully accepted, and their daughter Beryl married Edward Ives, the only surviving member of a "real Hennage family." Through her husband she is well positioned to take an active part in the core group, but owing to a slight sluttishness and overreliance on her mother's support she has never become more than a potential member.

Ethel Crowe is another fringe figure, never accepted by the rest of the village. Having married the son of the local builder whose wife came from a "real Hennage family," she alienated herself by her aspirations and her never-failing spite. She is now widowed and has become totally isolated except for her next-door neighbor, the good-natured Mrs. Howell.

The last of these fringe figures is Mrs. Cushing, a member of a third-generation family which had no links of kinship with any other core-group member; I have never got the impression that they ever really fitted, but this is hearsay. If Mrs. Cushing ever was a potential core-group member, she forfeited advancement by precipitating the divorce of the local tenant farmer and staying on as his "housekeeper" which, it is implied, covers the usual multitude of sins. The rest of the villagers have no structural position; one or two are influential through personal friendship with a core-group member, but it must be stressed that this is due only to personality. No structural principle is involved and their influence is never direct, only through a core-group member.

So far I have shown that a core group exists and I have defined it in village terms. Membership is dependent on genealogical[11] or affinal[12] connection, residence, and competence.

---

[11] Genealogical: By blood by either paternal or maternal line.
[12] Affinal: Through marriage.

2 / The individual life cycle

By following an individual through his life cycle it may perhaps be easier to understand the reactions of a "real Hennage person" to the outside world. Of necessity this life cycle is theoretical, as it has been constructed from the structurally significant events in the lives of many individuals. Those nearing the end of their lives were children before World War I, and those who are now children are growing up in changing situations. Events in their lives will appear to be very different, but it seems possible that the underlying attitudes will not have changed. Almost all incidents have been interpreted with hindsight, for it is impossible to see something and to decide immediately what relevance the incident has for Hennage norms. I find myself in a somewhat similar position to Turnbull among the Mbuti, except that whereas Turnbull could at least watch the Mbuti in the forest, I can only observe the effects of norms and attitudes consolidated inside the home.

For convenience I will follow the life cycle as laid out in Figure 2.1 This not only gives the life cycle but also provides alternative choices which have an effect on the completion of the cycle as a potential core-group member. I will start at birth, although this is arbitrary, for the cycle is a continuous one, the position of the parents having an effect on the child, and vice versa.

BIRTH AND BAPTISM

The first assumption must be that at least one of the parents is a "real Hennage person"; it does not matter which, since membership can be conferred through the male or female line. Similarly, it does not matter whether the child is male or female. The fact that there is a child at all is the relevant factor, and provided the parents' union is stable, legitimacy does not matter either. Shortly after birth a first child must be baptized. Baptism is one of the rites of passage that "real Hennage people" must pass through, and it is at this point that the nuclear family of husband, wife, and child is socially recognized. All children are baptized, but the first child is baptized quite soon after birth, certainly within the first year, whereas subsequent children

28

are frequently older. The ceremony is attended by as many members of the wider family as can be gathered together, and this includes members of the family who reside elsewhere. Although the Book of Common Prayer lays down that baptism should take place in the presence of the congregation, this practice is rarely observed, and the service takes on a distinctly familial aspect. With later children baptism shows even less observance of Christian orthodoxy; the usual practice is for these other children to be baptized at a time convenient to the family, irrespective of their age. Thus Desmond Clare's eldest daughter was baptized within a year of birth, but his later children were baptized all

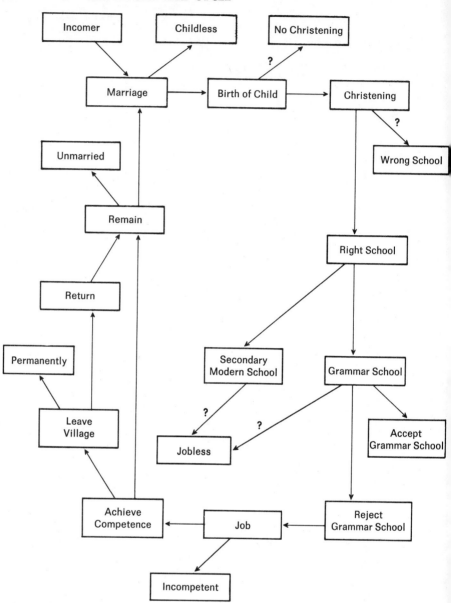

Figure 2.1—Diagram of observable criteria for core-group membership. This diagram only shows the basic *requirements for core-group membership; influence within the group depends on other factors.*

together when his eldest son was eleven, his second daughter was seventeen, and his ninth child was under a year. There are few families with enough children to demonstrate the tendency as dramatically as this, but it is noticeable that second and subsequent children are baptized later. That this was the usual practice in the past can be seen from the parish baptismal registers.

Another interesting feature is that nonresident families, that in other circumstances would be members of the potential core group, make an effort to have their children baptized at Hennage. Iona Thomas, née Clare, brought her eldest child to be baptized, and some years later her other two children were baptized at Hennage with their cousin. Similarly, Ransome Clare's great great grandchildren are brought up from Bristol to be baptized and to see their great aunt Alice Dyball, Ransome's daughter, as well as their various Clare cousins. The Lovage family also did the same in the past, and the register records several baptisms for families who have now vanished, including one Alice Sabina Goose, who married an Italian, went to live in Italy, and then returned to have at least one of their children baptized in Hennage. The pattern is the same—the first child is baptized singly and soon after birth, the rest in a bunch.

SCHOOL AND AFTER

For the child the next structural event of its life is to go to school. They all go to the school in the next village, which is the school for Hennage. After primary school there is a great divide, secondary modern or grammar school. There is only one of each for the area, so there is no choice once selection has been made. Only four children in recent years have gone to the grammar school, all the rest going to Burgh Secondary Modern School. If a child goes to the latter there is no problem; but to go to the grammar school causes difficulties. As I mentioned earlier, education is not thought to be very desirable, so to go to grammar school at all is an implicit rejection of village norms. For this reason the histories of children who have gone to grammar school are revealing.

The first to go was Iona Clare. According to informants she had always been "stuck-up" and ambitious, so that no one was surprised when after school she took a clerical job in a national firm in Norwich and married an ambitious young railwayman from Burgh. According to the criteria of the core group, she could come back and be a "real Hennage person," but her career would seem to preclude any return for her on her own terms, so the question should never arise. If she returned she would be accepted as a "real Hennage person," but her influence within the core group would be limited by her acceptance of and adherence to village norms. Her younger sister Evelyn followed her to grammar school, but unlike Iona, Evelyn hated it from the start and eventually left under a cloud, as I mentioned in the previous chapter. This cloud was fairly irrelevant to the villagers, though they bore it in mind for future use. The important point was that Evelyn had rejected grammar school and by doing so had reaffirmed her adherence to village norms, and on her marriage later she was on the road to becoming a true core-group member. Her subsequent misbehavior and social decline has other roots as far as the village is concerned.

The third child to go to grammar school was Brian Hoveringham, whose father, a farm laborer, was ambitious for his son. Brian's mother was herself debarred from full core-group membership by her adherence to the chapel.

Brian's future is hypothetical. Having done very well at grammar school and narrowly failed to get a place at university, he now works as a meteorologist at a nearby R.A.F. station while still living at home. His position in the village is anomalous; he has clearly rejected the village by adopting what villagers see as an aberrant attitude toward education, but equally clearly he adheres to the village by continuing to live there. The test will come when he marries and in his subsequent career. Until then the village maintains friendly but neutral relations with him. This attitude is compounded by his unmarried state—in village eyes he has not reached social maturity—and by the fact that he is almost the only young man of his age in Hennage and therefore has his friends outside the village. In addition, he is a competent violinist. This is an example of changing behavioral patterns, for many of the older core-group members played instruments at one time, but now the interest is viewed as abnormal.

The fourth and last child to go to grammar school was Elizabeth Cushing. I am unclear as to her position vis-à-vis the potential core group, as she married very shortly after leaving school and went to live in Sett. The spending of early married life away from the village is not uncommon and need have no effect on her social position should she return.

What would have happened had Brian Hoveringham gone to university I do not know, but it is unlikely that his work would allow him to continue to live in Hennage. Nobody from Hennage has ever gone to university. If further education takes place, it is at King's Lynn Technical College or through an apprenticeship, usually arranged by Burgh Secondary Modern School. Of the two young men who have recently been to technical college, one has now left the village with his family. The other is Kenneth Dobson, an electrician, who is now married, with a small boy, and well on the way to becoming a member of the true core group. The question of further education does not arise for most young men, since on leaving school their first interest is getting a job. At this stage it does not matter much in relation to their status within the village what sort of job they find, although the young men often state a desire for a skilled job. Later on when they marry the type of job is important for status in some degree, although it must be remembered that in most of the jobs available there are skills which can be demonstrated to one's fellows even if the job itself is not classified as "skilled" by the Registrar General. What happens if a man cannot get a job at all, I do not know as I have not heard of a case in Hennage. For girls the situation is slightly different. No girls have ever received further education, although it is the ambition of some to become fully qualified hairdressers, an occupation which entails apprenticeship. Frances Lowe thus qualified by working in Sett. At this stage the type of work done becomes subsumed under the general heading of competence. There is a degree of status dependent on the type of job, especially for the men. For example, a straight laboring job at a factory or road-sweeping is not high in status, although this does not necessarily bar the individual or his family from taking a full part in the life of the core group. However, all the people who have or have had low-status jobs are incompetent in other ways as well, so it is difficult to apportion the causes.

MARRIAGE

By this stage the young individual should be a potential core-group member, and the next step is marriage. There have not been enough marriages during my time in the village to say whether there is an optimal age or not. The only indication I have on this is the situation of Thomas Lee. Now that his mother has died he has been able to buy the former police house and is said to be looking for a wife. The village finds this amusing, as he is fifty-one and is clearly regarded as too old for marriage. Within wide limits the choice of marriage partner does not matter much provided that he or she is roughly of the same background, age, is competent, and is prepared to conform to village norms. The partner certainly does not have to be from the potential core group, and indeed such marriages are relatively rare. Marriage takes place in church, almost without exception. Evelyn Clare is the only person I know to have been married at the Registry Office, and this was in deference to her father's anticlericalism. Only two members of the potential core group actually in Hennage have been married in all the time I have been there. One marriage took place while I was away. The marriage I was able to observe was between Noreen Dobson and Andrew Howell of Sett. As far as the village was concerned, the wedding was a family affair and only relatives and a few close friends attended. An exception was Muriel Clare, whom I know was not invited. A few middle-aged women waited outside the church but did not enter. Andrew Howell is a driver-salesman for Corona Soft Drinks, a perfectly respectable job, particularly as his father is the Corona manager in Sett. His family are Sett people, so if they decide to settle in Hennage he should have no difficulty in becoming a member of the potential core group. This is what happened when Frances Richardson married Peter Lowe, a Sett man, and they found a house in Hennage. Marriage seems to follow no pattern on viri- or uxorilocal[1] lines—residence after marriage being determined by where the young couple can find a house. Usually marriage is deferred until a house has been found, and as this is done through the network of both sides, it is likely that the house will be found near the residence of the bride or the groom.

It is uncommon for a couple to live with either set of parents, and I know of only two cases where this happened. In both cases the marriages seemed to have been forced, owing to the pregnancy of the girl. The first was Evelyn Clare, who married Richard Stevens. The couple lived with Muriel Clare, a situation that was considered highly unsatisfactory by both parties even though the cottage was redivided into its original condition of two one-up and one-down cottages. As soon as there was a house available in the village Evelyn and Richard Stevens took it. The second instance was Errol Dobson, Noreen Dobson's brother, who lives with his mother-in-law at Sheringham: This situation is complicated by the fact that Errol and Wendy are not actually married. Her mother refuses to give her consent—it is said because she finds her daughter's unmarried mother's allowance too useful to give up without pressure. However, the point of the story is that Errol lives with his "wife's" people.

Perhaps the most important aspect of marriage in this context is that it is still only potential as far as the village is concerned. The final step is a child. Frances Lowe shows this clearly. She had been married for some years before the birth of her first child and had been a mild, unassertive young woman. When the baby arrived she became much more assertive and is now well in evidence among the younger members of the core group. Symptomatic of this change in status is the way in which she is referred to by third persons; from being "Frances Richardson, married to the Lowe boy" she has become "Frances Lowe, Richardson as was." This is not to say that marriage as such is unimportant; the unmarried can never become members of the effective core group. Tom Lee is socially unimportant; Fred Clare-Hoveringham is very rarely seen in the village; and the Hoveringham siblings, Horace, Gwen, and Eric, play no part in vil-

---

[1] Viri- or uxorilocal: Virilocal, living after marriage with the husband's family or in his village; uxorilocal, with the wife's family or in her village.

lage life. However, to be married but childless is also difficult to carry off successfully, and the only person who has succeeded, at least in part, is Alice Dyball, who by a combination of personality and relatives managed for a time.

CHILDREN AND UPBRINGING

Having acquired a competent spouse and a child, the next step is to bring the child up according to village standards. Not to do so is a reflection on one's competence. Muriel Clare stumbled over this. Evelyn was not blamed for the scandal in which her behavior landed her—the responsibility was laid firmly on her mother's shoulders and it was her mother who lost status. The same lack of competence was demonstrated by Maud Clare-Hoveringham in her treatment of her son Tom. There are numerous instances of gossip concerning the upbringing of children. Lucinda and Justin Goole, for example, are constantly criticized for the "neglect" of their children, but this criticism is in terms of the different patterns of child-rearing in different social groups, for the Gooles are young middle-class incomers who have a boutique in Norwich. From birth until

There is little place for retired men.

the child is adult this cycle continues with any deviation on the part of the child being explained as incompetence on the part of the parents. When the child reaches adulthood and marriage the parents abdicate responsibility. If the child does not marry or is childless, this does not reflect on the parents. Harold Church, for example, has lost no status because his son Thomas is childless. However, if all a couple's children leave the village, there is some loss of influence.

DEATH

Having settled the children, life flows on smoothly for the individual, provided he demonstrates competence and continues to adhere to village norms. During this period death is of paramount importance, not only to the individual but also to the spouse. The manner of death is all-important. There are three significant types—death from old age, premature death, and suicide. From an anthropological point of view, the first is least interesting. Death of the old is normal and expected, old in this case being defined as over seventy, although death over sixty-five is only slightly premature. To have survived so long is a mark of competence, and death is eventually the fate of all: in this case there is little avoidance of the kin of the deceased. Avoidance is marked, however, if death is premature and unexpected. When Fay Dobson's husband Harold died aged fifty-four, she was avoided for weeks. If she went into the shop, she was always served ahead of her turn. If she was already in the shop, people would wait chatting outside until she left. Villagers would go indoors when they saw her coming down the street—not abruptly but tactfully, as if they were about to go in anyway. If a meeting was unavoidable, there would be the minimum of conversation, simply "Good morning" as they passed. This went on for some eight weeks after Harold's death, gradually diminishing as time passed. Similarly, Muriel Clare was avoided after her husband died in his early fifties. In her case total avoidance was not possible because she was the postmistress, but there was a distinct easing off of custom.[2] The death of a child has the same effect on the parents. Perhaps this avoidance may be seen partly as a reluctance to be associated with incompetence as well as delicacy and respect for the grief of others.

The avoidance of the kin of the deceased varies according to the degree of kinship. Spouses are avoided most markedly, as are the parents of a deceased child. Children of the deceased are less sharply avoided, and for a shorter period. Thus while Fay Dobson was avoided for about two months, her son Kenneth resumed normal social life after about four weeks. Siblings do not seem to be avoided much, at least not if the deceased is a brother or sister-in-law. On Charlie Nobes's death, his widow Hannah was avoided by her own sister Joan, who was not herself avoided, at least as far as I could observe. In-

---

[2] Easing off of custom: There was a distinct drop in the amount of trade.

deed, Hannah Nobes received support from Muriel Clare, herself a widow, rather than from her own family.

The most interesting type of death is suicide. I have never been in the village when there was a suicide, so I do not know if avoidance of kin is practiced. However, the only true comic stories are told about suicide. They are recounted with enormous admiration and much mirth. Interestingly, the personality of the suicide is forgotten and only the fact that the person committed suicide is remembered. "Farmer Fred" Hoveringham committed suicide early this century; nobody can remember why. Neither can they remember who he was, and there are no Fredericks or Alfreds in the Hoveringham family in the registers. Apparently he drowned himself in a water butt—and "Ooh, his sister did get a turn when she saw his legs sticking out at the top," they say, wiping tears of laughter from their eyes. A similar story is told of the two Rust brothers, Herbert and Pecker. The neighbors heard a drumming on the partition wall of their cottage, and when they went round they found Bertie hanging from the beams. They cut him down and went through to the back kitchen where Pecker was washing up. "Pecker," they said, "your brother's hung himself." "I know," said Pecker, "he said he were going to." This last line is told amidst gales of laughter, but when I asked who Pecker and Herbert were, nobody could remember. There are three Rust brothers in various registers at the right date (about the early 1920s), but there is no Herbert, and Pecker was a nickname and no one could recall his real name. The only other funny story concerns a man whose name is variously remembered as Miller or Moore, and no one remembers who he was at all. He did not commit suicide physically but socially. At the date of this story, 1912, the field opposite his cottage was a lake. Something went wrong with the drain, and this, combined with heavy rain, caused the lake to flood, bursting across the road opposite his house. As the water flooded in through the front door he took up a sledgehammer and in desperation knocked a hole in the back wall of the cottage to let the water out. The point of the story is that he knocked the hole right next to the back door, which he had not thought of opening. Everybody laughed at him and about him to such an extent that he left the village. This is a left-handed story which shows the opposite face to the suicides proper. It is similar in its application; suicide is memorable and funny, and clearly has a deep meaning. I will discuss the interpretation of these stories later.

Whatever the mode of death, burial follows. Again there is one exception— the anticlerical Basil Clare was cremated. If the funeral is of a core-group member, all core-group members go, as do many incomers. Nearly all send flowers, mostly wreaths, and a great deal of money is spent on this display. After the funeral everybody goes home. There is no wake or funeral tea, not even for relatives and close friends of the deceased.

However, this is not the end of the individual. A lavish memorial stone is placed on his grave, and this will be tended and fresh flowers laid as long as any of his descendants in the direct line remain in the village. This duty certainly goes down as far as grandchildren, but whether further is uncertain. The old gravestones now are so worn as to be illegible, and though some of these graves are tended, I never have been able to determine whose they are. One other possible memorial is worth mentioning; this is in the giving of Christian names. There is some tendency for names to be handed down, especially if the original recipient was a forceful character. Thus the Clare family always have a Ransome, although I do not know if our Ransome was the first Clare to bear the name. Similarly, the Hoveringhams had Esau and Jacob for elder sons for generations until recently, and other families show the same pattern, though less markedly.

The life cycle of an individual is, then, fairly closely circumscribed by core-group norms if he remains in the village and is to be an effective core-group member. It is largely by observing the results of transgressions of norms against observable status that a "typical" life cycle can be built up.

3 / The core group as a unit

THE CORPORATE NATURE OF THE GROUP

So far we have assumed that the core group is in fact a corporate group[1] that has definite criteria for membership and methods for recruitment all maintained in an idiom of kinship. As well as kinship residence within Hennage is a necessary condition; and for effective membership of the core group a certain degree of competence, as it has been defined earlier, is required. From the point of view of the core group, its major function is to maintain itself. Its members see themselves as forming the base of a social hierarchy, the hierarchy itself being part of a wider system of which they are fully aware, though regarding it as irrelevant to village life. This hierarchy is best summed up in the progression villagers to gentry to landowner, as we mentioned earlier in our model. This view is conceptualized in the idea of "place." Each level of the hierarchy has its own "place" in the social structure, and between these levels there should be reciprocal functions if the system is to work to the benefit of all. In a system of this sort there must be mediators to effect these reciprocal functions. I am concerned in this study with the articulation between gentry and villagers and, therefore, with the mediator between them. It should be made clear that at no time has there been a direct confrontation between villager and landowner. In Hennage the mediator is the Vicar, who is appointed by the landowner. In the model it was suggested that the tenant farmers could also be mediators, but all the evidence tends to show that they have acted only as economic mediators between the landowner and their own employees, never as mediators for the village as a whole. Because the core group is a self-maintaining group any factors impinging from the outside world are interpreted in their own terms and incorporated into the system, for unless this can be done the system will no longer function; and if the system cannot function, the core group would no longer exist. Therefore core-group members have a vested interest in maintaining the system; they will of necessity select their social facts from the situation in which they find themselves. The situation is obviously capa-

---

[1] Corporate group: This is fraught with difficulties. I am following Fredrik Barth's use of the term (see *Nomads of South Persia*, cited in Recommended Reading). I use the term to mean a self-perpetuating group, aware of themselves as a group in relation to the outside world and acting, at least to some extent, as a differentiated social unit vis-à-vis other similar units.

ble of many interpretations, and the one chosen will be dependent on the attitudes and values of the groups concerned. These attitudes and values can be illustrated from the memories core-group members have of their historical past and are corroborated to some extent by written records.

THE TRADITIONAL POWER STRUCTURE

Since 1710 the Stamfords have owned the vast majority of the agricultural land in the parish and have appointed the most important and permanent of the middle-class inhabitants, the Vicar. Every job was ultimately at the mercy of the landowner, and such has been the solidarity of the gentry that to be thrown out by one of this group made it difficult to get work on another farm or estate. The choice for the villagers was, essentially, acquiesce and remain or rebel and leave. As indicated in the model, the only power structure was a vertical one running from landowner to gentry to villagers. With the coming of the railway it might be thought that the economic domination of the landowner was challenged; in fact it was not, as Lord Stamford built up such a large moral debt owing to him from the railway company that he must indeed have appeared to have remained omnipotent. Not only was he a large shareholder in the company but it was coal from his northern estates that the railway largely depended on. Beyond this he made available the land on which the railway junction and works were built after the company failed to obtain its original choice of site. He also provided land for the railway company's housing and built many of the houses himself, providing all the bricks from his own kilns. He was in a position to impede the progress of the line, but in fact he expedited it. At about the same time, the Local Government Act, creating the alternative structure of the County Councils came into force. This too might have weakened Lord Stamford's political position as the apex of the hierarchy, but the *de facto* head of the Parish Council, the local representative body of the County Council, was the Vicar. The traditional power structure was composed of three discrete social groups arranged in a hierarchy with a single mediator. The new power structure is still hierarchical, but is composed of representative bodies incorporated into one representative group (Figure 3.1).

It may be in order to give here a list of work opportunities open to core-group members (and others) in Hennage.

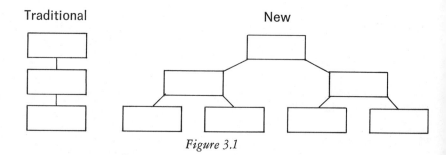

Figure 3.1

1. In the prerailway period occupational opportunities were agricultural laboring, crafts dependent on agriculture, crafts dependent on people (building, tailoring, cobbling), and house or garden servants to the gentry.

2. When the railway flourished and gave work to two thirds of the male population, opportunities were available for agricultural laboring, crafts dependent on agriculture, crafts dependent on people, house and garden servants to the gentry, and, of course, railway work. Fewer people were employed in agriculture by now, and while the railway encouraged a wholesale meat business in Hennage, grazing and butchering store cattle do not demand much labor except on rare occasions.

3. Since the closure of the railway and continuing up to the present, work has consisted of agricultural laboring, agricultural service industries and service industries dependent on people, now including electricians, television repairmen, and shop assistants, as well as the traditional skills of building and joinery.

There has thus been a continuous movement away from agriculture, from railway work to the service industries dependent on agriculture which now employ the majority of Hennage inhabitants. This move away from direct agriculture clearly weakened the structural position, at least in the economic and political field, of the landowner. In the past the immediate employers of the villagers were themselves directly dependent on the landowner, but now this level of the hierarchy has increased and become more diversified. But in a social sense Lord Stamford is still the apex of the hierarchy as far as the village is concerned.

CONTINUANCE OF THE TRADITIONAL STRUCTURE

The present social structure is partly straight tradition, for little has happened to cause the villagers to change their views. Indeed, historical events have been incorporated into the mythology of the villagers, thus reaffirming the social system. This is illustrated by various stories still widely current in the village concerning actions of past Lords Stamford. During the building of the railway an incident took place that is still remembered and told with relish. A laborer was walking home from the railway across a right of way through the home park of Burgh Hall. He had just climbed over a stile and was a few yards further on when a voice behind him ordered him to return and open the gate. The voice belonged to the then Lord Stamford, who was on his horse. The navvy[2] turned and said he'd be buggered if he would, whereupon Lord Stamford said, "Do you realize who I am? I am the owner of this land." The navvy replied that he didn't care, owning the land didn't make him his superior. Lord Stamford, now beside himself with rage, claimed that it did indeed make him his superior as his ancestors had fought for the land. The navvy turned back right quick at that, saying, "If you get off your horse, I'll fight you for it all over again." Lord Stamford declined and galloped off. This shows the attitude of the landowner clearly enough, but the village attitude comes from the gloss that they add every time—"The navvy was an Irishman;

[2] Navvy: An unskilled heavy laborer who worked on the building of canals and railways; derived from "navigator."

his Lordship thought it was one of us." For the villagers this is a joke against Lord Stamford. No villager would have dreamed of answering his Lordship in such a manner, a fact which his Lordship didn't apparently know.

Evidence of the landowner's behavior is not confined to the distant past. As recently as the late thirties the then Lord Stamford used to ride around his estates on a white horse, lashing out with his whip at anyone who did not raise his cap or show suitable deference in other ways—or so it is said—to the great surprise of respectable middle-class retired people. Even nowadays the dowager Lady Stamford comports herself in a manner suitable to a grande dame and, expecting instant compliance with her wishes, usually receives it. On the other hand, the present Lord and Lady Stamford are very rarely seen in the village and seem to play no part in the village mythology. This idea of a village mythology will be developed later. For the moment it should be realized that the social behavior of past Lords Stamford has taken on a mythological aspect for the construction of attitudes toward the apex of the inclusive hierarchy for the core group at the base.

MEDIATORS

I have noted that Lord Stamford appoints the Vicar of Hennage, and this appointment gives the Vicar a structural position in the social system as mediator between the village and the landowner. The Vicar has a structural role to fulfill, and how well he fulfills it may be measured by the memory of his incumbency among the core group. Of course, the longer the incumbency is held, the more possible it is for the Vicar to fulfill his role. That the Vicar is seen by the village to have this structural role can be seen by the concept of "place," which is strongly held by the core group. "Place" is reciprocal within the system between the village and the Vicar, both as the agent of the landowner and as *de facto* chairman of the Parish Council, or in his position as mediator between the village and the outside world. Structurally the Vicar represents the village to the outside world and the outside world to the village, traditionally as the agent of the landowner, who had his own structural position as the apex of the hierarchy of which Hennage was one of the bases, this hierarchy being included in the wider system of county and country. The most important fields for activity imposed on the village from outside are local government and education, and these have become subsumed into the traditional system through the structural role of the Vicar.[3] The Vicar is the *de facto* chairman of the Parish Council, whose members are in theory elected by the villagers from members of the village. The Vicar, since the local state primary school is a Church of England school, is also chairman of the board of governors, the other members being local tenant farmers and members of the middle classes. The other field of importance for the Vicar is as mediator and organizer for village social activities, such as fêtes, clubs, dances, and similar activities. It is the Vicar's "place" to organize and initiate the activities wanted by the

---

[3] Vicar: The minister of the Church of England responsible for the parish to his patron and his bishop.

village and the villagers "place" to support these activities. The core group conceive of this as a reciprocal system. It is the "right" or "place" of the Vicar to initiate action within the village either from internal village needs or from the needs of external agents. The village has a "right" to expect such action to be more or less acceptable, for it is their labor that supports the hierarchical system, and it is their "place" to accept such action (or lack of action). This concept of "place" is widespread in any hierarchical society, but in Hennage it seems to have two meanings. The first, and normal, meaning is that it is not correct for someone of a subservient group to display initiative; it is not such a person's job in the total social hierarchy. Second, "place" has a meaning in terms of members of the small-scale social group—it is not the "place" of core-group members to represent that group to the outside world, for by so doing they would destroy the corporate nature of the group.

MEDIATOR OLD STYLE

The Vicar with the most prominent place in the mythology of the group is the Rev. Samuel Owens, who was the incumbent from 1896 to 1941. His behavior seems to have been in sharp contrast to that of the present incumbent, the Rev. Kenneth Shepherd, and it is the contrast, continually commented on by members of the core group, that may give us an understanding of the structural position of the Vicar in this particular subsystem. Not all villages which have a predominantly rural proletarian population are organized in this way; it just so happens that Hennage, through the chance of the landowner appointing the Vicar, is.

The Rev. Samuel Owens, having been the incumbent for nearly fifty years, had a good chance of being remembered by the core group. Of the three incumbents between the Rev. Owens and the Rev. Shepherd, core-group members have no memory of two and of only the personality and the film shows of the third. The Rev. Owens seems to have acted in what would now be regarded as a highhanded way, but he is remembered with great affection. I think this stems from the fact that he fulfilled his structural role, although I cannot give a detailed account of the various ways in which he did this. I can only suggest that he did so, first from the fact that he is remembered as having done so by members of the core group, though they express it in the terms of, "Ah, Mr. Owens, he were a proper old Vicar"; second by various written records such as lists of the Parish Council members, the minutes of the Parish Council, and the school log book; and third by the villagers' memories of what Mr. Owens did. It is an account drawn partly from mythology, partly from written records, and partly from memories of other village events that are indirectly relevant to this matter. I have no guarantee that this is what actually happened, but it is what members of the core group remember as happening, and this I believe is relevant to an anthropological analysis.

First, let us examine the Rev. Owens' role as mediator between the village and the outside world as expressed in his position as the *de facto* chairman of the Parish Council and as the chairman of the board of governors of the school.

Throughout his incumbency he was the *de facto* chairman of the Parish Council; other more or less permanent members were the tenants of the two largest farms, and the other two members were either the smaller tenant farmers or entrepreneurs—in any case members of the middle classes. This restricted membership was challenged for a brief period from the early twenties to the middle thirties by members of the core group as a direct response to trade union activity. The last member of the Parish Council from the core group resigned in 1936. The reason for the resignation is always given as, "The council didn't do anything we wanted . . . they always outvoted us." If pressed for details of "they," the Vicar and the tenant farmers were always cited. Since then no member of the core group has shown any interest in the affairs of the Parish Council, or indeed behaved as if it were relevant to the life of the core group. It would seem that the attempt by the trade union to get leaders or representatives of village opinion onto some official decision-making body failed in Hennage by the structural nature of the village. The middle-class tenant farmers, led by the Vicar, opposed the views of the core-group members, and given this opposition, the core group simply opted out, leaving the Parish Council to the Vicar and the tenant farmers once more. I do not know what the issues were that divided the Council; there is no indication in the minutes, and the only person who was on the Council at that date and still remains in the village is old Harold Church, who cannot remember. He does not think there was any particular issue—"They just didn't want us there." He was also very clear that it was a union decision that working-class members of villages should try to become members of the Parish Councils, and that in Hennage there was no pressure from inside the core group itself for membership on the Parish Council.

On the other hand, the tenant farmers and the Vicar did not always present a united front. From the minutes of the board of governors of the school in the early years of the Rev. Owens' incumbency—up to World War I—there were frequent rows between the Vicar and the tenant farmers over the question of children being excused from school attendance in order to work on the farms for seasonal needs, such as stone-picking and hay-making. (Norfolk school holidays have always allowed for harvesting.) The school takes the children from four villages. Two of them, Hennage and Massingham, are characterized by the predominantly rural proletarian nature of the population and the other two by a population including a high proportion of independent small holders. The log book indicates that it was always the children from Hennage and Massingham who were rowdy, inattentive, failing in their standards, and absent, usually to work on the land or to look after the younger children while their mothers did. The largest tenant farmer, who employed the vast majority of the children, was himself on the Board of Governors. The farmers had resented the Education Act of 1870 on precisely these grounds, and when the villagers saw that the governors themselves openly defied the law, it is hardly surprising that they should have considered the landowner, the Vicar, and the farmers to be more important than the officials of an outside bureaucracy.

It was in the school that the Rev. Owens demonstrated one of his most memorable instances of highhandedness. In those days, the spelling of surnames was not standardized—it is not consistent even now. A boy named Charles Mears had won a prize at school, and the prize was a book, suitably inscribed, handed to him by the Vicar. According to the inscription, it had been won by Charles Mayes. When the boy ventured to mention this error, the Rev. Owens fixed him with his eye and said, "If I say it is spelt M-A-Y-E-S, that it is how it is spelt," and from then until the family left the village, Mayes the name remained. When I said I thought that perhaps the Rev. Owens had exceeded himself, the complacent reply was, "That's the way it was in those days; if Mr. Owens said 'Jump' we all jumped," as if it was his right to make decisions for members of the village.

Social life within the village flourished during his incumbency. Although the population was slowly declining, there never seems to have been the noticeable imbalance of age groups that there is now, so there were people to partake in social activities. Members of the core group recall asking the Rev. Owens if they could have a cricket club. Permission was granted, with the exception of play on Sundays, and a suitable meadow was found with the cooperation of a tenant farmer. (The common had not then been leveled and was open land, bumpy and overgrown, on which people let their hens run, grazed a goat or donkey, and sent their children to play.) The core group recall dances and whist drives held in the Vicarage Rooms that the Rev. Owens closed sharp on midnight. "He used to come in, put out the light, and that'ud be it; home you had to go then." Church fêtes are remembered as being vastly superior to the present ones, with everybody in the village going, and much of the organization being carried out by members of the core group under the eye of the Rev. Owens or his daughter. Sunday school was active, and outings for the children were arranged to the sea in the summer. It is said that everybody went to church then, and that those members of the village who belonged to the Methodist Chapel (now closed and converted into two cottages) attended church in the mornings and chapel in the evenings.

The Rev. Owens was obviously a memorable figure, and indeed one old man still dreams of him. The affection with which he is remembered is enhanced by the memory of his daughter. Miss Owens bought up village houses as an investment against her old age, and when she died in the middle fifties, left them to the tenants, thus substantially increasing the number of owner-occupiers. From what members of the core group say about her, she seems to have behaved like a Vicar's daughter in Victorian fiction, being sensible, tolerant, and compassionate and reflecting well on her father's image. Both fulfilled the village ideal of how a Vicar and his family should behave.

Obviously, too, the Rev. Owens contributed to the maintenance of the traditional structure; indeed, he could hardly have done otherwise. As Lord Stamford's appointee, he must have accepted such a system; otherwise, why should he have been appointed? And having been appointed, he had to continue to uphold the system. Given the existence of the system and its acceptance by its constituent units of landowner, gentry, and villagers, the system can work if all units fulfill their roles. It is with a Vicar who does not fulfill his structural role that we are now concerned.

WHEN MEDIATORS FAIL

Why the Rev. Kenneth Shepherd does not fulfill his structural role I am uncertain, but it is perfectly clear that he does not do so in any sphere except the spiritual one. (For example, once a month he takes Communion to an elderly housebound parishioner who is working class but not a member of the core group. The core group themselves seem totally unconcerned with their spiritual welfare.) He holds the position of Vicar, but he does not behave in a manner concomitant with the holding of this position. That he does not fulfill his role is most apparent with regard to the activities of the Parish Council and with regard to village social life. His position as chairman of the board of governors of the school is only marginally illustrative of his nonfulfillment of his structural role, but his behavior here is interesting for its own sake. When I carried out the survey of village attitudes toward education, mentioned in the Introduction, the headmaster of the local school was very interested and wanted to see the results. One of the questions I had asked was, "Would you like more, or less, contact with the school? And if more, what sort?" Nearly everyone replied in the affirmative, and the most popular sort of contact wanted was to spend some time actually in the classroom situation "to see how things have changed." The headmaster was very interested in this response and arranged for any parent to stay at the school for a day or part of a day, but if he or she wanted lunch to let him know the day before. A notice to this effect was sent home with each child; only one request was made, by my wife. It was not as if the school was difficult to get to; most mothers walked or cycled the distance twice a day, and few mothers were working at that time of year. There was no reason why they should not have visited the school, but no one did, even though it had been their own idea. In part they had been hoist by their own petard, as they should not have given the answer they thought I wanted in the first place. But they had seemed genuinely excited and pleased by the possibility of visiting classrooms, a practice which had taken place in a few schools in the county at about that time and which had been reported in the paper and on the local television news. Perhaps they did not feel that it was their place to visit the school. Had the Rev. Shepherd interested himself in the survey, which he knew about since he was one of the parents interviewed, and encouraged the acceptance of the headmaster's offer, more might have been achieved from the headmaster's point of view. Apart from this little is known about his activities as chairman of the board of governors, particularly as the whole system is under review.

With regard to his role as chairman of the Parish Council, since the resignation of the last core-group member from the Council, vacancies have been filled by the co-option of middle-class incomers by the Vicar. The only two permanent members are the Rev. Shepherd and Mr. Evelyn, the tenant of Hall Farm. In 1960, the first election was held in thirty years, because two middle-class incomers wanted to become members and there was only one vacancy. The village took a keen interest in the proceedings, and there was much discussion as to the relative merits of the two candidates. Feeling appeared to run high. Polling day was eagerly awaited, and when the result was announced it had clearly been a close fight. The winner had won by three votes out of a total vote of eleven. No member of the core group had voted; they had talked about an interesting and amusing piece of news, but the election was irrelevant to their lives.

More important, the Vicar in his capacity as chairman does not encourage public attendance at Parish Council meetings, and indeed does not publicize the date or place of such meetings or the decision reached. This attitude on the Vicar's part is best illustrated by the decision of the Parish Council to close one of the two rights of way in the parish. The right of way was closed ostensibly on the grounds that it had not been used for twenty years. No one on the Parish Council was in a position to make this assertion, not having been in the parish for twenty years. In any case use or nonuse is not a sufficient reason for closure, I have been told. What the real reason was I have no means of knowing, but the fact that the land-owner planted a copse for the protection of young pheasants across the right of way just before the closure may be suggestive. No attempt was made to find out the truth of the assertion, and the right of way, in fact, has been and still is used frequently, almost daily. I am very unclear as to how people knew of the closure, for there was no notice in any very obvious place, and I myself was told by the shopkeeper. When I inquired of those members of the core group I knew were in the habit of using it, I found that some of them did know it had been closed. However, they still continued to use the path, with no sense of defiance or bravado; it was simply as if the decision was irrelevant. They did not go to the Vicar in his capacity as chairman of the Parish Council and ask on what grounds the closure had been made, either singly or as a body. Whether the core group would have made any efforts to protest or to get the order rescinded if the order had been enforced I am unsure. Judging by a similar case in a neighboring parish, it is probable that a compromise would have been reached, which in this particular case means the barbed-wire remains across the opening to the path, but being well covered with polythene sacking, one can easily climb over or through.

It had been emphasised repeatedly that the right of way had always been there and that the people had always used it. As I was also in the habit of using it, I asked the Vicar the date of the next Parish Council meeting so I could attend and raise the matter. It was impossible for me to attend on the chosen date, but I gave the shopkeeper, who was sympathetic but pessimistic, a statement with arguments to read on my behalf. This he did, but the only people present were the Vicar and Mr. Evelyn, as no notice had been put up to advertise the meeting, contrary to procedure. Foreseeing this possibility, for the meetings of the Parish Council are never advertised, I had already written to the County Council, which despite the Vicar's assertions to the contrary, showed a lively interest in reopening the right of way. There the matter rests at the moment.

It can be seen that representation upward is being blocked by the mediator who is not fulfilling his role of representing the core group, as a corporate group, to the outside world of authority. No core-group member could have tried to circumvent the Vicar in the way that I, as a middle-class outsider, was able to; nor could he have applied to Mr. Evelyn as the Rural District Council representative of Hennage, as they did not know that he held this position. In either case it would have been taking over a representational position, which would have destroyed the role of the mediator and the structural relationship of the group to this role. As villagers themselves have said, in this and other instances, it is not their place to initiate action; it is the place of the Vicar to do this. My action in writing to the County Council direct to reopen the right of way, thus bypassing both the Vicar and the tenant farmer, is tacitly approved of—mostly, I think, because it is regarded as "one in the eye" for those in immediate authority. The whole question of whether the right of way stays closed or is reopened seems to be totally irrelevant, since if people want to use it, they will.

One of the most striking examples of the lack of communication between the Parish Council and the village arose over the application of a film company to the Parish Council for the use of the common for the cricket match scene in Joseph Losey's *The Go-Between*. When villagers learned on the local television news that a rent had been settled upon for use of the site, they were furious. They didn't want unseen cash for the Parish Council, they wanted parts as extras—particularly as the news report had said that local people would be needed as extras. The arrangements for the casting of extras went wrong, however, so that by the time the Hennage people arrived at the hall in Sett, all extras' parts had been allocated to Sett people. Upon hearing this the Hennage party, led by Joan Thurlow, left in high dudgeon. The obvious person to mediate on their behalf was the Vicar, but nobody went to him. Maybe it was assumed that he was opposed to them, since he had accepted the film company's offer for the common without any consultation or even communication with the village. Instead, hints were dropped in the village shop that non-cooperation on the part of the village was to be expected, and mutterings of sabotage were heard by the shopkeeper. Since the action of the film takes place during the turn of the century, television aerials were going to have to come down, cars reparked, and traffic along the road halted during shooting. In their threats of sabotage the villagers were being entirely realistic; a policy of simple but thorough noncooperation would have made filming impossible. The villagers seemed to feel that they had a moral right to the parts as extras, given that such parts were available, since it was Hennage common that the film company was using and they were Hennage people. All these hints and threats were carefully couched in the third person, none being attributable to any one individual, but they were so constant that the shopkeeper felt compelled to mention the dissatisfaction in the village to the Vicar. This, as he well knew, was precisely what had been intended. Whether or not the villagers would have carried out their threats never arose, as more parts were created after the Vicar talked with the film company. This was the method employed by one section of the core group, the Dobsons predominating. Another section, the Clares, attempted the same tactics of carefully contrived hints in the third person to me, as they knew I was friendly with someone employed by the film company, whom I eventually approached. Which channel worked I do not know, but all those who wanted parts had parts in the end.

Having finally been offered parts, a small section of the core group, among whom Joan Thurlow and Alice Dyball were noticeable, wished to refuse these parts, apparently on moral grounds. A larger part of the core group, mostly younger and centered around June Thurlow, wanted the parts as extras whether or not they had been obtained by blackmail. Eventually, Joan Thurlow repudiated her moral high horse and accepted a part, along with an extraordinarily high proportion of her relations. Alice Dydall did not accept a part and, as far as I know, never mentioned the film again. It is interesting that Joan Thurlow maintained her high status among the core group in spite of her inconsistency in behavior. It would seem that a willingness to join the majority position is more important within the group than to stand by an individual position.

This is one of the few occasions on which the core group acted in a corporate manner. That the core group is a corporate group is clear from its insistence on a consensus about any action the group might take and by its dependence on a mediator to represent it to the outside world.

CLUBS, SOCIETIES, AND CONCERTED ACTION

There are at present no clubs or societies in the village. When I first arrived there was a bowls[4] club. Anyone who wanted to play could join, and administration seemed to mean those who wished for a game scratching their heads for another person they could persuade to make up the game. This was the end of a series of once-flourishing clubs—cricket, football, and darts as well as bowls. Their demise seems partly to be an effect of the population imbalance existing in the village and partly of a reluctance on the part of the Rev. Shepherd, and to a lesser extent of Mr. Evelyn, to fulfill their traditional roles as organizers of such clubs. For clubs to function it is necessary to have the people take part in them, and in Hennage at the moment there are not enough young men to make up a football or cricket team. For darts and bowls it is necessary to have a room; these used to take place at the public house, but this has now been closed. Even if there were the age groups to support cricket clubs and dances, it seems unlikely that the Rev. Shepherd would organize them. That the villagers could not organize them themselves is clear, both from the example of the fête I organized and from a consideration of structural principles—it is not their "place." No members of the core group, as far as I know, take part or belong to clubs based in other villages.

One positive action for which the Rev. Shepherd was responsible was the clearing and leveling of the common into a playing field. It seems that this was done in response to a request from the cricket club of the day, which was dominated by the family of the local dairyman. The family, though employing many people from Hennage and being connected by marriage to the Hoveringham family, live in the next village, and because of their entrepreneurial status its members are regarded and treated as middle class. The labor of stone-picking was done by village women, who claim openly that they were not paid, although Mr. Evelyn and the Rev. Shepherd, as members of the Parish Council at that date, claim they were. Since the disappearance from the village of young men prepared to play football and cricket, and with the dispersal of the dairyman's family, which coincided with the arrival of a large number of very young children in the village,

---

[4] Bowls: A game of skill played between teams on a lawn with weighted wooden balls (bowls). The object of the game is to get one's bowls nearest the jack, a little white ball.

members of the core group have been complaining about the leveling of the common and expressing their wish to have old common back. "Ah, we used to play on the common for hours when we were little," they say, "but these won't." And someone else always says, "Yes, but it's so cold now they've cleared it, and there's nowhere for 'em to play. We had all those little old hillocks and bushes and things. Oh, we could have a rare old time over there." Their dissatisfaction is blamed on the Rev. Shepherd yet again, though it is difficult to say with how much justification. The impression gained is that there was little if any consultation with the village and an overdependence on the views of the dairyman, William Hastings, who was himself on the Parish Council at that date though resident in another parish.

OTHER MEDIATORS

It is apparent that Hennage relies on mediators between itself and the outside world in nearly every sphere of life. Even when the opportunities for direct action between individuals within the group and the outside world exist, Hennage people prefer to use a mediator. Shopping is done primarily in the village shop, and for other needs there are regular deliveries to the village by two butchers, a fishmonger, two mobile grocers, an ironmonger, and a coal lorry. There is also a monthly visit by the mobile library. All of these services are well patronized. For clothes and shoes the villagers prefer to use mail order, although they are aware

The shopkeeper in his role as mediator explains social security benefits.

that in many cases the quality is inferior and the price higher. This attitude seems odd, as there are not only adequate clothing and shoe shops in Sett, but Norwich with its well-known chain stores and market is hardly beyond reach, particularly as all members of the core group have a car or access to one. The village shop is also the post office, so pensions, benefits and insurance stamps, and advice on how and when and what to claim can all be obtained from a known mediator. All members of the core group watch Anglia television and take the *Eastern Daily Press* for their newspaper (with the exception of Gregory Dobson, who returned to the village only on his wife's insistence, and the Lowes, who take a national paper and then exchange with Frances' grandparents who live next door.) National news seems to be discussed only within a local context, such as the level of unemployment in East Anglia or the decision of German brewers to buy or not to buy Norfolk barley. Other news which has no local context is rarely discussed, and if it is, it takes on a somewhat fairytale quality. I have been present when news from Ulster was being shown on television and there was no response at all except in the most conventional of phrases. It would be interesting to see if this attitude has changed now that the East Anglian Regiment has been posted to Northern Ireland.

EMPLOYMENT AND EDUCATION

Only five men in the village work totally outside the village context; the rest work in the locally owned dairy, a village-owned joinery, the village garage, which is also an agricultural contracting business, or on Hall Farm. Of the five only one works for a large company of road engineers as a laborer, and the others work for small local firms in Sett, mostly builders. The only real exception is Brian Hoveringham, who, as I mentioned earlier, works as a meteorologist with the R.A.F. To the best of my knowledge, none belongs to a trade union in more than a formal manner, if at all.

The villagers send their children to school because to do so is easier than not to do so, and, more important, they want their children to get "a good job"—meaning a skilled or semiskilled job. At the primary school level the children enjoy attending and there is little absenteeism. The feeling changes when they go to secondary school, where there is considerable absenteeism, particularly among the girls. Carol Thurlow is at home more often than not, and Noreen Dobson "felt faint" so frequently that she became a by-word in the village. This is not discouraged by the parents; if a child does not want to go to school he does not go. It appears that whereas boys can see some relevance between school and job, girls find the connection difficult.

THE LAW

On occasions there is the law to contend with, but this is rare. The Hoveringham family, as joint owners of a cottage, were taken to court for letting the house after it had been condemned as unfit for human habitation. The villagers were

Young farmworker—one of the few. Most of his contemporaries work in agricultural service industries.

sympathetic on the whole, but condemned the family for drawing attention to themselves. The most frequent recourse to law is after a death, when it is usually discovered that the deceased left no will. In this case a lawyer must be called in if real estate is involved. This is known to be an expensive and cumbersome process, but wills are rarely made, presumably because the deceased wished to avoid voluntary contact with the law—after all, enforced recourse to the law can hardly affect him. The only other occasions when the law has been invoked have involved incomers and the control of dogs; and in one case it was only the threat of the law. The Gooles are middle class, boutique-owning incomers from Hampstead who owned a dog which bit, in quick succession, the postman and Frank Richardson. The latter threatened to call the police unless the animal was kept under proper control. This was, I think, a pure threat, but Justin Goole, rather than risk further alienation of the villagers (they were unpopular already), had the dog put down.[5] The villagers were wholly on the side of Frank Richardson in this matter and felt that he had acted correctly. The second case involved Mrs. Clare, whose dog bit

[5] Put down: Destroyed by a veterinarian.

Kenny Adcock's dog in the course of a fight. Kenny Adcock called in the police, which the villagers quite explicitly believed was going too far. He was well aware that Mrs. Clare had no control over the beast, even on a lead, and that she took the animal out only at well-known times. The episode caused maximum ill-feeling, entirely due to the fact that the police were called in. Many people had complained of Mrs. Clare's dog, but Kenny Adcock did not play the game according to the rules. The only other case that I know of where the police were called in also involves Mrs. Clare. This was the occasion when her daughter Evelyn was out all night with several young men when she was only fourteen. Mrs. Clare was unequivocally condemned for calling in the police, especially as the situation was seen by the villagers to have arisen entirely through her own incompetence, and she lost a lot of status as a result of it. The only situation within the core group concerns the late Harold Dobson, who was notoriously light-fingered and was regarded as disagreeable into the bargain. The degree of his unpopularity might be gauged from the fact that very early on, before his death, I was told the story of how he had shot a nightingale because "it made too much bloody row." He was known to take sacks of corn from his then employer for his rabbits, but this was regarded as fair game. However, he did not stop there; in the words of one informant, "He'd take anything as wasn't nailed down," and it got to such a point that men slept on their allotments[6] overnight to prevent his ravages. Yet there was no question of calling in the police, and as far as I can make out, this course of action was never even contemplated or discussed—the villagers simply increased their vigilance. Apropos of crime, I visited a former village policeman who has now retired. He had no cause for reticence, for his wife, a Hennage woman, is now dead, and he no longer has any contact with Hennage. He confirms the picture that the police are involved only with great reluctance by recalling that his time in Hennage had been very restful and he never had more than an occasional out-of-date license and the odd stray dog to deal with. Nothing else whatever was brought or came to his notice. This corroborates the fact that core-group members keep internal disputes and dissensions within the core group, for this policeman knew nothing of Harold Dobson's depredations, although he was stationed in the village at the time. It must have been a well-kept secret, for Harold Dobson's staying at home "because of his bad back" became renowned throughout the village as a portent of a series of daring daylight raids while the men were at work, and the women and children rushed to guard the allotments and gardens—or so the story goes now.

I have shown that the core group is a corporate group, but to a large extent a closed group, with members taking what they are offered by the outside world on their own terms and manipulating that which is imposed on them so that it becomes consonant with their own system.

---

[6] Allotments: During World War I agricultural land near the village acquired by purchase or gift was allotted to members of the village for the growing of vegetables as part of the war effort. The allotments have been in use ever since.

4 / Sanctions, ritual, and myth

SANCTIONS AVAILABLE

The most frequent way in which members of the core group act is against someone within the core group who has transgressed a norm. This may seem an outrageous statement, but the whole pattern of Hennage social life is composed of the interlocking minutiae of everyone's observable behavior. Every time two or more members of the core group are gathered together the meeting immediately takes on the air of a postmortem in which every fragment of knowledge about the past twenty-four hours is gone over in detail. The knowledge thus garnered is carefully evaluated and stored in terms of village norms for redissemination at the next meeting. Three points can be made about such a system. First, it is clear how gossip spreads; the second point is less obvious but more interesting. While everyone is silent about their companions of the moment, they are nonetheless evaluating every detail of each others' attitudes and potential standing within the core group based on what they are saying, how they learned it, what they are wearing, what they were doing in the street at that particular time, and so on. Their views about each other are retold, with gloss, to the next person met. To illustrate how this system operates, let us consider Mrs. Richardson's "linen line" (clothesline). This is well positioned for maximum observance, and Mrs. Richardson is usually the first to get her linen out. Any deviation from this routine arouses speculation in every observer's mind: Is Mrs. Richardson ill? or her husband? or her daughter or grandchild? Am I to congratulate myself on being particularly early? But if I am early why is Mrs. Thurlow even earlier, which is not normal? Is she going currant-picking? if so, with whom? Or is she just going to Hunstanton for the day? Or was Carol sick during the night? These and a host of related questions are raised. The third point is that this is the mechanism by which norms change; they change according to the social material available. This is a difficult point to document, since as I am not a member of the core group I am not included in gossip; I therefore have to work from old gossip and observation. One example of a changing norm that I can give from observation, though hardly structurally significant, is the size and shape of the drawers worn by the women of the village. These are now briefs, and it has been fascinating to watch the gradual spread of these exiguous garments from June Thurlow's linen line to practically everyone else's. This observation is not as silly as it sounds, for a woman's linen line is meant to be seen and commented on because it is one of the major expressions of competence for a woman. (Mrs. Richardson even goes so far as to put her ironed linen out to air just outside her front door.)

GOSSIP

The effects of gossip are very difficult to see, for they show only over a long period of time. Obviously, major transgressions have a more rapid visible effect; examples of these were given earlier in the histories of core-group members, notably that of Muriel Clare. In Hennage there is nothing like a council which hands down a ruling concerning an individual's deviant behavior, and no single person, representative, or group has any authority to make a judgment in this area. This means that sanctions must be diffuse and, it would seem, depend as much on the individual's awareness of his transgression as on the awareness of the rest of the group. The social interaction between core-group members is of such a nature that an individual could impute a number of motives to any action taken in relation to himself by another member of the group. Which motive is chosen by the individual member must depend on the state or condition that the individual believes to exist between himself and the group as a group. Just as the group acts against an individual member who is thought to have transgressed, the individual member also must act in relation to the group. His action can take only one form if the individual is to remain an effective member—tacit acceptance of the group's gossip and ostracism leading to a more acceptable mode of behavior. Other alternatives, such as defiance or avoidance, only serve to isolate the individual within the group. The sole agents, then, that the group has at its disposal are the diffuse sanctions of gossip and ostracism; but owing to the layout of the village, gossip travels relatively slowly and ostracism is only observable over a period of time.

The transmission of gossip seems to be casual, though not quite as accidental as it appears at first sight. An important feature is that the village has no center or forum where everybody meets; it does not even have the central common surrounded by cottages so beloved by the writers of detective stories. Therefore gossip is primarily passed on during journeys up and down the street, to the shop, to borrow a knitting pattern, to get eggs or vegetables, to take the washing in or out (many cottages have their gardens and linen lines in little clusters, not necessarily adjoining the cottages), to see Mum, and so on. Before the coming of mains water, the series of pumps and wells scattered up and down the village may have been gossip centers. Another change in the transmission of gossip has been the passing of the paper round into noncore-group hands. When Grace Bishop had the round, she took between four and five hours to deliver the papers from one end of the village to the other, and it was a useful means of gossip dissemination, a fact she was fully aware of and cherished. After her death, Muriel Clare took over the round for a while but then suffered a stroke and gave it up; now the papers are delivered before nine by the shopkeeper in his car.

Exactly what form the gossip takes I am not sure, for people tend to break off when a noncore-group member comes into earshot. But judging by what has been told me by core-group members about past gossip, the corpus of the material is formed by the bare facts, general opinion, and related behavior remembered from the past. The network the gossip follows is not, within the core group, of any structural interest, as it seems largely to depend on whom the individual bearing the gossip meets. As the core group is so small and as its members are all related, the information can follow virtually any channel. This is not to say that gossip dissemination is completely haphazard; it is fairly generally known who goes to the shop or to visit their parents or children at what time, and one's own timing depends somewhat on this information. I cannot give chapter and verse for this, as I was never completely abreast of gossip by the very nature of its dissemination, and core-group members may calculate the timing of their movements to avoid outsiders just as much as to coincide with each other. On a grosser scale I could observe it. For instance, I was aware that at 10:30 on a Tuesday morning it was likely that the only person in the shop would be Maud Lee. Everyone else was aware of this, which is why she was alone there. Similarly, Mrs. Clare took her dog out at certain hours, and as she was totally unable to control this sizable beast, the street, or at least our end of it, would be deserted from the time she set out until the time she and the dog returned. As I have said, the finer points of the system escaped me, but it is clear that avoidance and meeting are not wholly accidental. There is a sense of disappointment if no one is met on the way up to the shop, as if something of almost ritual importance had been missed. This may indeed be the case, for it is by this apparently casual intercourse that cohesion is maintained among core-group members, and if one meets no one it may be because one is being avoided or ostracized. This will become clearer when the effects of gossip are considered.

The transmission of gossip is not confined to the core group. It reaches other individuals in the village and members of other villages, although by this time gossip is no longer an agent of structural alteration, or at least only to a very secondary extent. That this is so is a reflection of the structure of the core group. This is perhaps easiest to see in terms of networks. Within the core group the concept of network hardly applies, for each individual is linked to every other by a multiplicity of ties—genealogical, geographical, friendship, and so on, and the mesh is so dense as to make the concept redundant. Outside the core group, however, conditions change; not only is genealogy a criterion for membership but residence as well, and no one, however well connected, can be a nonresident member. Conversely, no one can be a member, even if resident, without the necessary genealogy. Thus the networks emanating from the core group are personal and have no effect on the structure of the group. I have never come across any hint of a core-group member using his extragroup network to bring pressure on other core-group members. Thus anything that is said about a member of the core group by noncore-group members of the village or outside it is irrelevant to that person's status within the core group. The core group is a closed group, cut off from outside opinion, and however badly a member behaves, provided he remains in the village, he is still a member of the core group. His status is automatically higher than that of any incomers, and he cannot be denied his title of "a real Hennage person." This is not to say that interesting items of information are kept within the core group, but once outside they carry no structural implications.[1]

It is against this background that the nature and method of ostracism must be viewed. In the first place I have no evidence that ostracism is deliberate, and if ostracism represents a punishment for transgression or a mechanism for enforcing conformity, I am sure it is not so viewed by the core group, though it might well have this effect. Ostracism in Hennage is simply the corollary of conformity and egalitarianism. Where the average is so highly prized the company of the abnormal is not deliberately courted, so that ostracism becomes a by-product of a strict adherence to norms. Nor is this mechanism formal; it seems to result from embarrassment, not merely embarrassment stemming from association with the abnormal (which may indeed come into it) but also that induced by the difficulty of carrying on a conversation with an ostracized person. One of the features of gossip, in Hennage as elsewhere, is that the person who is being gossiped about can never be included in the audience of the gossipers and as that person is likely to be the subject of much of the conversation, an awkward pause is likely to ensue if he joins the conversation. If the person concerned has transgressed many norms, he is likely to be the subject of too many topics of conversation forbidden in his presence; to avoid embarrassment he is avoided. There is no suggestion of gossip or avoidance being used to enforce conformity or to punish transgressions or incompetence, it simply follows from the normal course of events. Not only do the members of the core group gossip about the individual member who has transgressed a norm, but the transgressing member is ready to impute any degree of isolation to the fact of his transgression. Thus each acts on the other; gossip, avoidance, and the perception of these by the transgressor are mutually reinforcing. Having said this, I feel that perhaps ostracism should be more tightly defined; the dictionary meaning is given as "banishment by consent: exclusion from society . . . ," but as I have shown, Hennage does not on this definition "ostracize" anyone. The individual is avoided, which gives the appearance of ostracism. There is nothing of the conscious motivation which ostracism implies; it is avoidance carried to its inevitable conclusion. The results of this avoidance are unattractive to a core-group member, and only three courses are open to him; he can reform, he can ignore the situation, or he can depart. None of these is wholly satisfactory. Reform is only possible over a long period—as in the case of Dennis Williams—and past events are always recalled on the occasion of a new transgression. Ignoring the situation means perpetual exclusion from the effective core group, while departure means finding a new house and possibly a new job, probably without the aid of one's normal networks of information. The only person I was ever aware of who left the village for this reason was the man who committed social suicide by knocking a hole in his back wall to let the flood water out.

Naturally, none of these courses is open to a bereaved spouse who is avoided, since the individual cannot change his or her state. Why then are these persons

[1] Structural implications: Relevant to the underlying social framework of the group. (See A. R. Radcliffe-Brown, *Structure and Function in Primitive Society*, cited in Recommended Reading.)

avoided? Two factors seem to enter into this. First, the normal course of gossip will tend to their exclusion, for the topic of gossip will be too embarrassing to them; and, second, their change of status produces—in the past far more than now —a structural alteration with economic consequences. Before the coming of pensions, a widower or widow, particularly with young children, threatened to become a strain on the families of the village. As no family was in a position to offer support for long, immediate sympathy was offered the bereaved, but further contact was avoided. This is illustrated by the history of Hannah Nobes. On the morning of her husband's death she was taken in by her niece, June Thurlow. This seems reasonable as June, or rather June's husband Fred, is the relative who lives closest, but it may be relevant that Fred and June had no spare bed so there could be no question of Hannah staying long. When evening came Hannah refused to spend the night in her house where her husband's body lay, and her attitude was regarded as perfectly reasonable in Hennage. She was not offered a bed in her sister Joan's house further up the street, where there were two spare bedrooms. Instead, she was taken down the street to Muriel Clare's. Mrs. Clare had a spare room, was a fairly recent widow herself, and had not sufficient strength of character to refuse the charge. Mrs. Nobes stayed for well over a fortnight[2] and was induced to return to her own house only when Mrs. Clare went to stay with her daughter in Peterborough—a visit she contrived as the only possible means of getting Hannah out of the house.

The change in economic status is not so marked nowadays, but the structural alteration is still relevant. A widow or widower is no longer part of a viable social unit and is therefore of less account among the core group with its emphasis on continuity. This concurs with the less strict avoidance of the recently bereaved old, who are hardly a viable unit anyway. There seems to be a definite feeling that an elderly married couple ought to die within a short time of each other, and in three instances this was mentioned in so many words. Given this attitude toward death, it would be expected that the death of a young mother or father would produce very strong avoidance, but I have no material to support this.

THE RITUAL OF SOCIAL LIFE

The core group, then, can be seen to act as a corporate group in order to maintain its own cohesion. Members see themselves as a group, as "real Hennage people" in relation to other villagers, to similar groups in other villages, and in relation to the outside world of "Them." The criteria for the recruitment, and therefore the continuance, of the core group are defined in terms of genealogy, residence, and to a lesser degree competence. The core group has its norms of behavior which center around the concepts of egalitarianism and modest competence. Potential members who find these norms unacceptable can leave the village and forfeit their membership. Similarly, those members of the group who contravene these

[2] Fortnight: A period of fourteen days; two weeks.

norms within the group—either by overcompetence or by incompetence, by trying
to exert authority or by being overdominated by some outside person or institution
—have the diffuse sanctions of gossip and avoidance applied against them, resulting in low status and little effectiveness within the group. In the discussion of
gossip, I have tried to show that the social interaction between members of the
core group has an almost ritual importance; the social interaction between one
member and another constantly reaffirms each member's adherence to the group,
like a constantly recurring communion service.

It will be apparent that I have used words such as "ritual" and "myth" without
being able to give an account of ritual acts or myths as such. To take ritual first,
the lives of "real Hennage people" appear to the observer to be affected by remarkably few ritual acts. They attend church only for rites of passage—baptism,
marriage, and burial—and the only other church services they take part in are
Harvest Festival[3] and Armistice Sunday.[4] They do not attend the great festivals
of the Church—Christmas, Easter, and Whitsun—which are attended only by
members of the middle class. How far Harvest Festival and Armistice Sunday
are canonical festivals is open to doubt. Harvest Festival is always held on a week-
day evening, never on a Sunday, and may be seen as a takeover by the Church of
the former Harvest Homes. Armistice Day I have no explanation for, except that it
is near All Souls Day. For the rest, I know that the church is dedicated to All
Saints, which is apparently the most popular dedication in East Anglia, and that
Hennage people remember their dead and take care of their graves. There are no
other ritual or symbolic acts that I have observed or been informed of.

It would seem that, for the core group, ordinary, everyday life *is* their ritual
life; everyday actions of social intercourse have their ritual meaning. This view of
ritual can clearly be seen to be derived from Leach (1954) and from the development of Leach's ideas by Barth (1961), though it must be made clear that I am
not suggesting they would endorse my view of Hennage ritual life. To give the
gist of my argument, I shall take Barth's definition of ritual (1961, p. 146):
"Ritual may be defined as the symbolic aspect of non-verbal action—those acts or
aspects of acts which *say* something, in terms of shared values and meanings,
rather than *do* something in terms of predictable material and economic consequences." The limitation to nonverbal puzzles me; conventionally ritual is action,
but I do not see why it should necessarily be so. In Hennage social life the
words are part of the action; if no words are exchanged, there will be no grounds
for social action. To continue with Barth's discussion of ritual (p. 147), it becomes
necessary to "look for further sets of acts, or aspects of acts, which carry and
communicate meanings in contexts vested with particular value." To me, it seems
clear that Hennage ritual life should be sought in the context of everyday social
life. Barth's Basseri nomads of Southern Persia vest "their central values in, and
express them through, the very activities most central to their ecologic adaptation.
This is perhaps possible for them only because of the picturesque and dramatic
character of the activities, which makes of their migrations an engrossing and

[3] Harvest Festival: A church service in autumn to give thanks to God for the harvest.
[4] Armistice Sunday: The first Sunday in November to remember the fallen of the two
world wars.

satisfying experience." Hennage people vest their central values in their social life, which is after all the only part of life left to a rural proletariat. It can hardly be described as picturesque or dramatic, but it is perhaps equally as satisfying and certainly as essential to the survival of the group.

MYTHS; CHANGE AND INCLUSION

Just as core-group members use their social life as ritual, so they seem to treat events that have taken place in the recent past which are part of their lives, yet outside, as forming a mythology. For a person to be included in the mythology he has to belong within the hierarchical structure of the system, yet by his behavior to have put himself outside the system. He is "larger than life" and therefore a myth-figure. Myth-figures reiterate the social values held by members of the core group by having overreacted toward these values themselves, either positively or negatively. This is particularly so for myth-figures from within the core group. At the moment, there are myth-figures at all levels of the social hierarchy. I have referred earlier to the fact that the stories concerning previous Lords Stamford have mythological characteristics which, concomitant to his Lordship's structural position at the apex of the hierarchy, emphasize his remoteness from the lives of the villagers. There are stories told about the gentry, too. These seem to emphasize the paternal quality of the structural position of the gentry as employers and mediators. They appear to be seen as father-figures, and there are no stories about members of the gentry which contradict this social image. This may be seen as a necessary corollary: if to fulfill one's structural role as a member of the gentry one is either a mediator or an employer, or both, one can only be seen as a "good" figure for the village. If such a member of the gentry does not fulfill his role as an employer-mediator, then he has no relevance for the villagers in a structural sense, and he is promptly ignored and forgotten. There are no stories about the "wicked squire." Similarly for the myths clustered round the figures of the past Lords Stamford; in order for the social system to function, Lord Stamford must seem to be as remote and as different from the villagers as possible. In terms of the social system it is perhaps necessary that the figure at the apex of the hierarchy should be seen by those at the base as opposed to themselves. Certainly in Hennage, the Lords Stamford are seen in the mythology as "inhuman" and "unnatural"—not in relation to their social equals, other apices of other hierarchies, but in relation to those at the base of his own hierarchy. There are also myth-figures among past core-group members. Prominent among these are those who committed suicide, and it is possible to discern a future mischief-figure in the person of Harold Dobson.

This brings me to a very interesting and somewhat puzzling feature. Of the myth-figures current among core-group members, all are assumed to have been real people, to have had a real existence in the historical past. There are no myths of a prehistoric past; in fact, there are no myths from outside the limits of a man's memory, which seems to reach back to four generations. I have relied for these stories largely on one informant, Harold Church. This is because Mr. Church was prepared and willing to spend hours talking with me, and his wife did not object to my presence. This last point is relevant, for Hennage people do not invite nonkin into their houses readily, and if they do the atmosphere tends to be somewhat formal and restrained. Neither is Mr. Church deaf, as are other potential informants, and while deafness can be overcome for a casual chat or occasional direct question, to have several long, tangled, and involved conversations is difficult. On the other hand, every story that he told me has been confirmed by other core-group members. Mr. Church's memory goes back to "things my grandfather told me," and as he is now over eighty, this period may cover one hundred and thirty years or so. Although all individuals mentioned in the myths are assumed to have been real people, members of the core group are not always able to identify these myth-figures in terms of real social identities. Examples can be seen in the stories of the suicides of "Farmer Fred" Hoveringham and of Herbert Rust; even the name of the social suicide (the man who knocked a hole in his back wall to let the flood water out) is not known accurately. This may indicate the importance of the individual's actions rather than his precise identification within the social system, assuming that for his actions to be socially significant he must already be contained within the system.

During my period of residence in Hennage, new figures have begun to creep into the mythologies. Whether previous myth-figures have been discarded during this period I am unable to say, but it may be expected that this takes place. The myths may be seen as a regenerative mechanism. They are generated by the system and are fed back to regenerate the values system in the same way that children provide the regenerative mechanism for the physical continuity of the system. The myth-figures are drawn from individuals within the system who can be remembered by other individuals in the system; they must have been real people. This "reality" ensures the validity of the myth for the system, and it is the system that equally ensures the validity of the myths. Why this reality should be limited to four generations is unclear. Some societies have oral traditions going back ten to fifteen generations, and these traditions are usually genealogical. This point may seem to have little relevance in a discussion of myth, but the genealogical traditions are historical events and can quite often be checked against outside sources. In Hennage the stories, though about people in history, that is, real people, are not themselves historical; it is the mythological content which is remembered and used by the core group. An example of such long genealogies may be found among the Bedouin of Cyrenaica. This society is structured from the base up into an inclusive segmented society, which may be expressed in the words of an old Arab proverb, "Myself against my brother; myself and my brother against my cousin; myself, my brother, and my cousin against. . . ." This means that for them any readjustment demanded by a changing situation at the lowest level of segmentation of minimal lineage[5] necessitates a constant manipulation at the point of articulation into the next inclusive segment. The genealogical depth for this minimal segment is three to four generations, and the articulator changes over time. The total tribal gene-

---

[5] Minimal lineage: The smallest social unit above the level of the nuclear or elementary family in a segmentary system.

alogy does not change and remains constant over long periods. In Hennage the nonoral tradition of the wider society provides the large-scale inclusive whole, so that the core group is only concerned with maintaining its own social identity. As with the Bedouin of Cyrenaica, this is done along the boundaries of the immediate larger unit—not in genealogical terms but in terms of the myths which validate the social system. Among the Bedouin of Cyrenaica, although change is occurring throughout the society, it is only seen to occur at the level of minimal lineages, the small-scale units making up the total society. The total society, as expressed in its genealogical charter, seems to change only very slowly. Similarly, Hennage is part of a wider society which, from the point of view of Hennage, seems to change in essentials very slowly. Hennage itself, in its own small-scale hierarchical subsystem, sees itself as changing quite fast. This change is in terms of the individuals and families who make up the core group. I have been told by several core-group members, "People used to say Hennage was all Dobsons, Durrants, and Clares, but there are not so many of us now. Other people come in." I must stress that this is not a comparison, simply an illustration to explain a point.

This change is more apparent to the outsider because the surnames change, as recruitment to the core group is often in affinal terms. There are very few members of the core group who have lived in the village all their lives, and members of other core groups from other villages in the wider subsystem often spend part of their lives in Hennage. This may make for some discontinuity in social tradition because there must be a constant reiteration of the facts if they are to be remembered within an oral tradition. It is only the behavior of an abnormal type that will be remembered in mythological terms; normal behavior is not the raw material of myths. This may give some indication of why I would expect that mythological figures current in the past in Hennage may have disappeared from among the myth-figures current now. That new figures become included in the mythology is clear. I have seen this happen to one man, Harold Durrant, who killed himself during the early years of my stay in Hennage, and it is in the process of happening to Harold Dobson. It seems that once an individual has put himself outside the system by physical death, or in a couple of secondary examples by social death, it is possible for his or her actions to become incorporated into the body of myth.

Of the stories which seem to carry mythological content, I will first consider those concerning the Lords Stamford. As mentioned previously, all stories relating to the Lords Stamford seem to emphasize the distance between them and the villagers, not merely a political-economic distance but also a social distance. The story of Lord Stamford and the navvy was recounted earlier. It can be seen, when taken with the village gloss, how nicely it illustrates the view of the social system held by the core group. So too does the story of the next Lord Stamford riding round his estates on his white horse lashing out with his whip at those who did not show him sufficient deference. It is interesting that both these stories, which have for their physical setting places where Lord Stamford, gentry, and villagers might all be reasonably expected to be, include an outsider so that the point of the story can be more clearly defined. The outsider represents the boundary between the systems. The navvy is clearly outside, for otherwise he would never have stood up to Lord Stamford the way he did. The retired middle-class

incomers who found themselves within range of Lord Stamford's whip illustrate
that while the villagers regarded his behavior as not unexpected and indeed suitable
to one of his position, those who were outside the system in which Lord Stamford
and the villagers were operating did not so regard his behavior. The third story
is of the then Lord Stamford who was making a bid for social prestige and held
enormous and glittering house parties at which the Prince of Wales, later King
George V, was a frequent guest. A popular form of entertainment for the house
party on summer evenings took place after dinner, with the ladies and gentlemen
taking seats on a terrace overlooking the garden. The servants were given lights
tied to long poles and were stationed throughout the garden in the gathering
darkness. The gentlemen, armed with shotguns and pistols, would try to shoot out
as many lights as they could to the applause of the ladies. This story is told with
great admiration, for Lord Stamford was behaving as a lord should behave. It is
in this story that the feeling of distance between Lord Stamford and the villagers
is greatest and there is no intrusion from their own world. Lord Stamford is among
his equals; and the servants coming from the estate villages may be expected to
have viewed the game in a different light. While Harold Church seemed to accept
the game as a game, Errol Dobson, a much younger member of the core group,
from whom I also heard the story, was shocked at the apparent callousness toward the servants.

Thus the myths concerning the Lords Stamford illustrate the social distances
between them and the villagers. The Lords Stamford are considered so different
as to be almost inhuman and unreal. This characterization by the villagers is
relevant to the discussion of art forms within the system, which follows in the next
chapter. It is immediately relevant to the attitudes of the core group to those in
authority. If social distance is emphasized to such an extent, if the apex of the
hierarchy is characterized in unnatural terms and those at the base of the hierarchy maintain and strengthen those characteristics in their myths, it would be
expected that those at the base will attempt to keep their distance from authority.
There are no myths or stories which illustrate any degree of closeness between
Lord Stamford and villagers and none that portray Lord Stamford in any very
human aspect. This emphasis on distance is taken to such lengths that I have
never been told by any core-group member that the present Lord Stamford lived
for a time in the village. I know he did, as he was still there when I first went to
Hennage.

It would seem likely that there are similar stories among the gentry which
illustrate their relationship with the Lords Stamford. I have been told one by Mr.
Evelyn, but as the gentry dependent on Lord Stamford are scattered throughout
the neighborhood and the only other representative is the Vicar, who is not a
storytelling man, this is the only example I have. At the time of the christening of
the present Lord Stamford's heir, the tenant farmers felt they ought to mark the
occasion with a suitable gift. Mr. Evelyn was chosen as their representative, and he
chose to give a silver tankard. Uncertain as to the form the inscription should
take, he consulted the dowager Lady Stamford. Summoning the butler, she had Mr.
Evelyn escorted to the silver vaults to see if he could gain any guidance on this
problem. Mr. Evelyn was surprised and depressed to see rows of silver tankards

presented to former Lords Stamford on similar occasions. He nevertheless went ahead with the idea, as it was quite clear to him that a silver tankard, while being completely redundant, was what tenant farmers gave. This story shows that the hierarchical nature of the relationship between landowner and tenant farmer is clearly recognized by both. The nature of the gift was irrelevant; that a gift was offered at all was the important thing.

The stories from the core group that are concerned with members of the gentry have a different emphasis in their mythological content and one that is again consistent with the relative positions of the gentry and the villagers within the system. The Rev. Owens, who fulfilled his structural role according to the highest of village expectations, has many stories which I have already recounted, all of which show the patriarchal nature of his role. The previous incumbent, the Rev. Cloudsley, also has his place in the corpus. He is remembered by a couple of the very old men for his cough mixture, which contained a high proportion of opium and with which he was remarkably generous. All swear that it was a very effective mixture, giving relief and a good night's sleep with pleasant dreams. A second story concerning him also relates to opium, for he was not only a generous dispenser but a generous consumer. On one occasion toward the end of his incumbency, he was so fuddled that he wrote the wrong names in the marriage register after a wedding. Doubting the validity of his story, I looked in the register, and there a year before he retired was an entry in very shaky writing, heavily scored through by another hand and with different names superinscribed. This was not held against him, it was simply one of his little ways. There were probably more stories about this engaging figure, for as Harold Church says, "Of course I can hardly remember him. I were only a little lad then, and he were an old, old man." But owing to the process of change within the village, the Rev. Cloudsley's other actions which may have given rise to myth have been lost.

Personal characteristics consistent with the position of the gentry are illustrated by these stories. Those of the Rev. Owens illustrate an autocratic nature, while those of the Rev. Cloudsley show a more benevolent one. Benevolence is also characteristic of stories about the Houghton family, who were the last tenants at the Hall to properly fulfill their role in village eyes. Benevolent and autocratic paternalism is how the villagers portray the gentry in their myth corpus, and this agrees with the structural role of the gentry as employers and mediators. It is their "place" to tell the village what action to take and the "place" of the village to carry out this action. In the stories of the Houghtons, this is what happens. The stories are all of a vanished, golden past in which everyone knew his place and the system worked to everyone's advantage. This is the overwhelming impression one gains from the stories relating to the Houghtons and the Rev. Cloudsley. Those relating to the Rev. and Miss Owens, while corroborating this picture, are more influenced by reality, for they are nearer to the present villagers in time. The Houghtons and the Rev. Cloudsley, being further away in time, are also further from reality. That core-group members know these stories are "unreal," that the content is mythological, is clear, for in the same conversation in which they evoke this golden past they will also say that people's lives were much harder then, food was poorer, housing was worse, that it was more difficult to get and hold a job, and so forth. There seems to be an implicit distinction between individual lives of members of the core group and their structural position within the subsystem which was then, at least in memory, in better working order.

SUICIDES

The speed with which an individual within the system can become embodied in the corpus of myth is illustrated by Harold Dobson and Harold Durrant. Harold Durrant committed suicide in 1966 and by 1971 he had become a hero. He was not a very popular figure in the village, moody and cantankerous. He had frequent and audible rows with his wife, his two daughters had both "married" Desmond Clare, and his son had "managed to get himself murdered" in a nearby market town, to quote my informant. He was an incompetent roadsweeper—obviously not a very competent character in the core-group sense. Then he committed suicide after a particularly loud quarrel with his wife. Nobody knows why, or if they do, they are not telling. I happened to be away at the time of the suicide, although I was kept fully informed by letter. In one letter I was told that he had shot himself in his own garden shed. Even by the time I returned two months later, the Harold Durrant I had known was disappearing. It is perhaps relevant that his wife moved soon after his death, and as the daughters had already moved to another village, the social unit to which he once belonged had disappeared. He is now talked about as having been a jovial old fellow, given to gaiety, a competent roadman with a witty tongue, and always out and around the village with flowers in his hat. This last is indeed true, but was not approved of at the time. Harold Durrant has undergone an apotheosis. He is no longer an individual, but a hero—and all because "He blew his head right off he did, up in the churchyard by his son's grave." It would seem that to shoot oneself on one's son's grave not only makes a better story but is more structurally significant than to do so in the garden shed of a council house. It reaffirms the primacy of the nuclear family, for without this one is already socially dead.

Harold Dobson seems to be in the process of undergoing a similar change. As will be remembered, he "took anything as wasn't nailed down" and had shot a nightingale, the first for many years, that was nesting at the bottom of the Vicarage garden, which at that point abuts onto the road. This nightingale features in many reminiscences, usually related to the tranquillity of the past before the road became so heavily used by motor traffic. It was, in a sense, a symbol of the golden past. The Richardsons in particular were enraged at the slaughter of the nightingale, for it used to sing just opposite their bedroom window, and although the event took place some twenty years ago, Mr. Richardson is still incensed about it. Harold Dobson died in June 1970, and already the stories told about him are beginning to change. There is now grudging admiration that anyone could be so unpleasant and self-centered, and he is clearly being cast in the role of mischief-maker.

The other suicides deserve some consideration. The first point that comes to mind is that they were all fairly incompetent in village terms. I have already illustrated the incompetence of Harold Durrant. Both of the other suicides were unmarried, and Herbert Rust was said to be "very difficult." Both lived in sibling units, not ongoing social units. Also of interest is that no woman is remembered as having killed herself, and this goes against the national tendency. It may be that women find it easier to succeed in their own sphere in this system. However, once having killed themselves, this incompetence is forgotten. Their personality is stripped from them and they become culture heroes, their exploits being recounted in terms of hilarity and admiration—the hilarity because they outwitted the system in choosing their own fates and admiration for their action in so doing.

As we have seen, the outside world is almost wholly irrelevant to the villagers, except as a parameter within which their lives are passed and over which they have little control. Those who become effective members of the core group fulfill themselves within their system. Those who do not and commit suicide, for whatever reason, stand a good chance of becoming culture heroes. In suicide they reaffirm their competence by deciding their own fate. It is interesting that those suicides outside the core group do not seem to enter the mythology. George Hardy, the last village shoemaker, hanged himself in his workshop. It is remembered when the house is being discussed, as it was when it was purchased by the Gooles. Mr. Hardy was not a core-group member and was unmarried, so his suicide is relevant to no one outside the system still living in the village, nor to the core-group members. He is virtually forgotten. In the same way, Walter Savory Durrant is forgotten. Although a Durrant on his mother's side, he was never regarded as a core-group member, for his parents never married or even lived together. His father just seduced his mother and that was all. And as his father was a Savory and therefore middle class, there were no pressures the core group could bring to bear upon him. Although Walter Durrant worked at Hall Farm and lived over the stables for many years, I had never heard him mentioned by anyone except by his employer in passing, until the morning of his death, when my wife, hanging out the linen, overheard the neighbors discussing it. The discussion took place in an atmosphere of considerable relief, as though a distasteful episode was finally closed. Nobody went to his funeral; the fact that he was dead was enough.

It can thus be seen that the myths reaffirm the nature of the system as perceived by the core group. Lord Stamford is viewed as omnipotent, remote, and almost unreal. The gentry are portrayed as father-figures. Members of the core group who have committed suicide, by putting *themselves* outside the normal in defiance of the system, become culture heroes. It must be emphasized that this is a construct of the anthropologist. There is no evidence that Hennage people regard the stories as consonant with the social structure of which they are part. By analyzing the stories they tell in relation to their social system, it seems probable that these stories can be regarded as myths.

5 / Art forms and social values

REAFFIRMATION OF GROUP NORMS AND OF SOCIAL AND GEOGRAPHICAL POSITION

Art in Hennage is strongly tied to the social values of the group, and turns on the twin foci of the individual within the group and the identity of the group itself within its wider setting. Art for its own sake is irrelevant to the core group, as is the abstract concept of beauty. In Hennage art performs a very direct social function. For example, I have never heard members of the core group say that something is of itself "beautiful"; their praise is always in terms of "that's a lovely bit of work." An object is valued because of the competence and skill which went into the making of it. It is judged on the basis of its functional craftsmanship and not its expressive content.

Many members of the core group have been in my house for one reason or another. After envying the height and size of the rooms (the drawing room and kitchen are converted from a former barn and harness room), they examine and admire the color of the carpet and the quality of the furniture, ignoring the pictures, of which I am quite proud and for which I have great affection. One of the local builder's men who was working in the house noticed that the pattern of the carpet was uneven and commented, "Must be a hand-made job." It was this builder and his men who carried out the conversion job on the house. I shall discuss this subject in some detail, as it seems to illustrate quite nicely the dependence of core-group art forms on an appreciation of competent craftsmanship. It was the first time these builders had worked with an architect, and they were doubtful about the success of this new departure until the architect showed them that he was prepared to defer to them on matters concerning the capabilities of the building materials, brick and flint. Within these traditional materials they knew their competence to be supreme. They were also using a particular sort of concrete block with which they were unfamiliar, and they laid these with the same care they had the flints and bricks. Bricklaying is a skill, one that most men in the village appreciate and had acquired to some degree, so that the care they used in the bricklaying was partly for their own satisfaction and partly so that their work should not be adversely commented on by others in the village. Many of the details in the house afforded them considerable pleasure, and when the electricians or the plumbers came, the builders would seize on them and show this

Fireback made at local foundry—set in wall as advertisement.

new audience the way they had cemented around the Aga cooker base, hung the doors (which were of a stable type and opened outward into the garden in their separate halves, thus apparently causing many technical problems), installed the clerestory windows in the bedrooms, and executed many other details of such a technical nature that I was unable to appreciate them. The house was originally built to follow the curve of the road, and none of the corners is a right angle, so the building of the stairs and later a dresser in the kitchen caused great difficulties. The solution of these problems gave them enormous pleasure, and they transmitted their success to other building firms in the area. Thus we find unknown plumbers, electricians, and so on, asking to examine these features if they happen to call at the house for any reason. The paintings and objects in the house that I would expect people of my world to comment on leave members of the core group cold. It is the details of craftsmanship that arouse their admiration or, on occasion, derision.

WOMEN'S ART FORMS

Art forms have different expressions for men and for women, reflecting their different spheres of competence. I shall deal with those of the women first, as the art forms of the men are more elaborate and lead into a consideration of past

Brick work windows in flint barn, 1760.

skills that are still valued. It may be said here that when I refer to art forms, I am dealing only with skills and not with traditional media of artistic expression. For Hennage people, however, the exercise of these skills is art.

The supreme competence for women is to be a good manager, and I feel that it is valid to see their account books as art forms. These account books are notebooks bought from the village shop in which they write down each purchase and its price, to be balanced at the end of the week against the housekeeping money given them by their husbands. Such lists of goods and figures seem hardly art, yet the pleasure of Mrs. Joan Thurlow, for example, in seeing that she is still within her limit is akin to the pleasure of a bricklayer in completing a well-laid course of flints. Other fields of competence for women of the core group, which may be regarded as art forms, are cooking, sewing and knitting, cleaning, and light gardening. Various women are known to be "good" at various things. Alice Dyball is famous for her wedding and christening cakes; June Thurlow "can knit anything"; Alice Richardson is a good seamstress; Evelyn Stevens is a very good cook. Indeed, when she left her husband he was irate to find that his girl friend could not cook, and he seriously expected Evelyn to come in during the day and leave food ready for them both. Mrs. Joan Thurlow takes considerable pride in her flower garden, as does Mrs. Huntley. In Hennage, women tend only the flower garden, with men responsible for the serious gardening. This custom is in contrast to that of the gentry in Norfolk, where it is the women who are extremely knowledgeable and skilled in this art. If this seems a rather meager list, it must be remembered that it is largely the women who take part in the ritual of social life, which in itself is a supreme test of competence.

Both men and women participate in the redecoration of their houses. Redecoration is frequent, and care is taken over color schemes for front doors, window frames, and curtains, which are hung with the patterned side to the street. The Richardsons and the Bishops are perhaps the most avid redecorators, but there are very few houses in the village that appear to be in need of redecoration. Most men do their own minor repairs, and some carry out quite major works; Mr. Richardson, for example, relaying all the downstairs floors quite recently and Tony Williams fitting totally new window frames. Even cleaning comes into this display of competence, and a clean and sparkling house is regarded by its inhabitants and others as "a pleasure to look at." Though it is frequently pointed out by herself and other female members of the core group that Hannah Nobes cannot sew or knit or even cook very adequately, "she can clean somebody else's house beautifully—she's really house proud for someone else." It is odd that while the men do the serious gardening, without exception they regard it as a penance, an attitude I cannot explain. Every person in the core group seems to possess some special little skill which, while it can be carried out by every other member, reflects on his or her individuality within the group. Thus, Charlie Nobes could "lay a grate like no one else; he'd have got a fire going while you or I was still getting the sticks." Frances Lowe, even before she became a fully trained hairdresser, was said to have "a way with hair." While these little skills for the women cluster round their traditional domain of feeding the family, cleaning the house, and washing clothes, the major skills of the men are focused round their jobs and the minor ones round the maintenance of house and car. Every summer evening and weekend, every little "loke," a driveway serving several cottages, is filled with the car, with its bonnet up and a group of men standing round.

THE SKILLS OF WORK

It is in their work that the men of the core group express their skills; the traditional fields of carpentry, bricklaying, and metal-working (which used to be done at the foundry and is now carried out at the garage) are seen as arts as well as work. This was also true in the past, when the multitude of jobs were subsumed under the heading of agricultural laboring. Ploughing, carting, mowing, hedging, reaping, thrashing—all these tasks had their skills, which were not only necessary for the efficient discharge of the work in hand but also maintained a man's individuality. As none of the workers on the farms in Hennage are members of the core group, and only two actually live in the village, I do not know whether the same situation prevails today, with the almost total mechanization of agriculture. It would seem likely that it does, for there are frequent tractor-ploughing and furrow-drawing competitions in the neighborhood. Ploughing matches involve ploughing a "stetch"—a strip of land computed according to the width of the wheels of the plough—whereas "drawing" involves one furrow only in terms of straightness—with measurements between the top drawers stated in terms of fractions of quarter inches. Many other competitions are held at the Royal Norfolk Agricultural Show, now permanently based just outside Norwich, which takes place for two days every year. This is a major event in the county, and all schools are closed for the duration. The competitions, which make up only a part of the show, are for tractor-driving, loading, sheep-shearing, and tree-felling, among many others. These competitions do not contradict what was said earlier about the distaste for competitive situations within the village. They are seen as being between villages, or farms, not within them. The winners are reported in the local newspaper and on the local television news as being "A So-and-so man, Mr. Blank," and this is also the manner in which they are discussed in the village. The continuity between the old agriculture of horsepower and the new mechanized agriculture is obvious if one considers the startling similarity between the care taken for the appearance of the tractors used nowadays in competitions and the reported pride in the appearance of a horse team in the old days. Indeed, the continuity is sharpened when it is realized that the parade of heavy horses is always one of the highlights of the show.

Members of the core group in Hennage are predominantly carpenters and bricklayers. Village bricklayers, over the generations, built most if not all of the houses in the village, and nearly all houses are marked somewhere with the builder's or owner's initials—they were often the same person—in intricate patterns. Although the houses are built more or less to the same design of two rooms downstairs, with a front door opening directly into the living room, and two rooms upstairs, or the alternative model of one up and one down, and of the same material, there are individual touches in their construction. These are particularly noticeable in those cottages built by the men who also owned them and were going to live in them. For example, although there have to be some bricks round the door and window frames of a flint cottage, the arrangement of these bricks is individual. Some cottages have a pattern of bricks among the flints of the gable, like a checkerboard, and the arrangements of the bricks in the gable tops themselves vary. Mrs. Euston's cottage, and the other two adjoining cottages that also belong to her, have a row of bricks halfway up the front, sticking out at an angle in a regular pattern, which is purely decorative. Most cottages have iron tie beams, which are essential to hold the walls together, but the tie plates are more elaborate than is functionally necessary. Some cottages have cast-iron decorated plates on their gable ends, which were cast at the foundry in the village before it closed in the twenties. Maud Lee's cottage, which belongs to the Hoveringham family, has a particularly fine example. Locke's Cottages, also owned by the Hoveringham family, whose members occupy three cottages out of the four, have a finely carved stone plaque giving the initials of the builder and the date when they were built. All the core-group men connected with building can tell who built a house in the village and when, as well as when and what alterations and repairs have been carried out and by whom. When I first started seriously interesting myself in the village and inquired where a certain person lived, I was always directed in terms of the details of the buildings, such as tie plates, and never in terms of the number of houses along the road. The churches and large houses of the neighborhood are known and appreciated in these terms. Each time a major repair is carried out on the church, the work is signed and dated in an inconspicuous place, and I have been told that on the roof of the church tower are the handprints or initials or marks of all the men who have worked on the church. Other structures in the neighborhood are commented on. On a neighboring

Pride in tools. The tractor is over six years old—contrast overgrown farmyard.

estate, there is a flint wall with brick pillars and coping running alongside the road for some three miles, built by Basil Clare among others. Whenever I have mentioned to Mrs. Clare that I have come back from Gland along this road, she always says, "Basil built that wall. He always said it was the best thing he did," and it certainly is a beautiful wall.

Consistent with the pride of core-group members in their work is their pride in their tools. Robert Crowe, the village builder who married the last female Rust, showed me his wheelwrighting tools; he is very proud of having been trained as a wheelwright, which he says is better than being a mere carpenter. Although he is nearly ninety, and the tools have only rarely been used since World War II, they are still well cared for. Old Mrs. Euston has kept her husband's tools and, indeed, still has his father's tools. Mrs. Clare very much wanted to keep Basil's tools, for they had been left on the building site. She says that Dennis Williams promised to bring them back to her, but when she opened the box it was empty. (To my knowledge, she has never taxed Dennis Williams with this but only complained about it to me.) Harold Church has all his tools, including the combined Vernier scale and slide rule he made himself. It seems as though much ritual importance is attached to a man's tools, symbolizing, as they do, his competence in his working life. There also appears to be a great pride in tools and machinery as such, complementing their symbolic value. There is much pleasure at the garage in being able to mend or modify a car without having to send away for a new spare part. For instance, when I had a minor modification made to a trailer, Percy Bigham, the garage owner, put far more effort into the comparatively simple operation than was necessary. This was clearly done not to please me but to satisfy his own sense of "doing a proper job." Relevant to this pleasure in machines is a story told me by Harold Church, which came up when he was telling me that he used to mend watches and clocks in his spare time. Apparently a lot of the old men in the village in his youth had saved to buy "turnip" watches, and it used to be considered a good joke for the younger men to ask them the time, knowing they couldn't really tell the time from a watch. When called upon for the time the old men would laboriously draw their "turnips" from their pockets, take a crafty squint at the sun, and say, "Reckon it's about half past twelve time." Although the watches were evidently status symbols, Harold Church emphasized that a part of the pleasure was in owning this complex and beautiful mechanism.

The foundry is commemorated in the name of the row of cottages that lead up to its site and in the name of the middle-class residence that has been converted out of it. At the entrance to the row of cottages are a pair of brick gateposts of an imposing appearance, with a collection of old cast-iron firebacks let into them and some iron plaques with Latin quotations cast on them. These gateposts are frequently commented on to middle-class incomers by members of the core group, who explain that the plates are firebacks especially cast as advertisement illustrating patterns the foundryman was able to reproduce. While the Latin is not understood, the lettering itself is appreciated, and several times people staying with me have been shown the gateposts. The gates themselves were bought by Lord Stamford for the Lodge at Gunton; and while the villagers are pleased that Lord Stamford wanted the gates, they would like to have them still in the village. On the other hand, one is not told about the gravestones in the churchyard. On the old ones there is a high standard of lettering and the shape of the stones is itself pleasant. It is said that the stone came over as ballast from Holland, as there is no native stone in the district suitable for carving. This may account for the lack of interest in the gravestones as an art form, although villagers will discuss flintwork in churches in detail and with great technical knowledge. Flint, wood, and iron are the material in which they work from choice.

EDUCATION AND CONTINUITY

The skills of the past are highly valued, partly for their own sake but more especially for their social relevance. To the members of the core group the past emphasizes their structural position around which they construct their value system. They seem to see in the skills of the past an opportunity to express their individuality yet within a system. Not only was their individuality expressed to their own satisfaction but such expression was appreciated or criticized within the group: it was a comprehensive system. It seems to be felt now that the traditions of these skills and the standards by which they were appreciated have been lost, and nothing has adequately replaced them. That traditional skills were in a constant state of change is conveniently forgotten, and the skills of a former technology are those of the golden past. The golden past is centered around the activities of Hall Farm, which seems to be placed in opposition to the railway, which once more was something imposed from outside. It is significant that the golden past at Hall Farm coincided with the advent of not only the railway, but also local government and the school, all symbols of a new order which was opposed to the old and necessitated its breakdown.

In spite of the golden past being focused around Hall Farm, there are remarkably few stories about agricultural pursuits. Apart from one instance when the use of sickles had to be reintroduced because of the state of the barley as a result of bad weather, the only story on these lines concerns the quality of Harold Durrant's work with the scythe—"He was a marvelous man with the scythe, you couldn't tell his cutting from a mowing machine. He cut it that close." Similarly, there are very few stories about animals. I have been told the number of horses used on Hall Farm, but only as an indication of the size of the farm, with no mention made of the quality or condition of the horses. Oxen were also kept, one yoke of them, but only out of deference to a very old man employed on the farm at the turn of the century or thereabouts who had always worked with them. My informant on this was trained as a shepherd as a very young man and is almost the only person in the village who admits to any fondness for animals. I cannot explain this dearth of stories about farming topics; perhaps it is because there is nobody now in the core group who ever worked on a farm. It would seem likely that competence could have been expressed through agricultural skills when

Gardening is an exclusively male occupation, but there is little feel for the land.

agriculture was the mainstay of the village. Since the coming of the railway, however, and more important now the service industries, competence is expressed in these terms, and it is these skills that are appreciated.

There are plenty of opportunities to see the skills and arts and crafts of the past in Norfolk. Of the four museums in Norwich, the Bridewell is completely given over to local crafts, and on the occasions I have visited it, has never been empty.

There are demonstrations of various traditional skills such as sheep-shearing, thatching, or horseshoeing at the Royal Norfolk Show each year. The village of Worstead (where the cloth of that name was originally woven) every year holds a festival that is devoted to the past to raise money for the repairs needed for the huge and staggeringly beautiful church built by the wool merchants. There is a "traditional" farmyard with young animals, displays of old carts and carriages, farm tools and machinery, vintage cars and bicycles. One can go for rides around the village in a steam bus, vintage car, or in a farm cart drawn by a carthorse. People from the village dressed in Edwardian clothes wobble past on early bicycles. In the same field in which the cars are parked there is a huge display of steam traction engines and thrashing tackle, and in the field across the road one can have teas and listen to the band while the children ride in old-fashioned swing-boats or the roundabout. The Worstead Festival is very popular, and although there are special attractions each day and evening for the three days it lasts, it is the long-term displays that attract a large number of people. In a village nearer to Hennage, there is a retired agricultural contractor who has collected steam engines and steam fair-ground organs. The barn in which they are housed is open to the public every Sunday afternoon and it is jammed. This is a popular outing for core-group members from Hennage. The atmosphere in the barn is cozy, and the red-plush theater seats are packed with old ladies knitting while gossiping with their neighbors over the deafening noise. Everybody seems to know everyone else, and old friends from other villages meet and exchange news between intervals of examining the organs. Many village fêtes have a display of "bygones," and they are always a success. At the fete I organized we had a display of old Norfolk postcards and objects I had collected from the Middle East, combined with teas. The exhibition was popular, and while people looked at the Middle Eastern things with some degree of interest, they were especially pleased by the old postcards of Norfolk.

It is interesting that at all these displays and exhibitions of old things, there are two attitudes that predominate. First there is appreciation of the objects on display: "that's a real bit of craftsmanship," they say, "they can't make things like that nowadays." They know what they are talking about. Errol Dobson displayed a surprising amount of accurate knowledge about the steam engines at Thursford and was the reason for my going to see them in the first place. People take a long time at items that interest them, and there is much discussion of the finer points, particularly among the men. The second attitude is reflected by the women. Every item they see in an exhibition of things from the past reminds them of a social event that took place in which such an item played a part. If the item is an article of clothing or a piece of household equipment, for example, the women will not comment on how well made it is but on who, of the people they knew, had one or used one and for what reason. It was the women who were particularly interested in the old postcards of Norfolk, and although some of the conversation I overheard was about how towns and fashions had changed, mostly it concerned with whom they had visited these places, on what occasion, for what reason, and what happened.

Traditional skills—pitchfork work.

SKILLS OF THE PAST

This interest in the past is fostered by the local paper, the *Eastern Daily Press,* and by the local television channel, Anglia. The *E.D.P.,* as the paper is known, carries frequent announcements about ploughing and drawing matches, agricultural shows, demonstrations of various skills, and exhibitions according to the season. There are some farms, notably on the fens, where horses are still used for certain tasks, and photographs of the animals working often appear in the paper. The captions below the pictures never comment on just the aesthetic pleasure or nostalgia evoked by the scene but also on the functional effectiveness of the farming technique that is depicted. One autumn I read in the *E.D.P.* that on a farm near us the corn was to be threshed by a steam-threshing machine—thrashing tackle, in the local phrase. I went with my children, and the yard where the thrashing took place was packed with people. They were not all middle-class individuals like myself, indulging their taste for nostalgia, though there were many expressions of regret that this method was no longer the conventional one. Many people near me were intent on explaining to their children how the tackle works and what skills are needed to keep the machine working at its greatest efficiency, as well as on telling them who, of their relations or friends, had worked with these machines. One farmer in a coastal village not far from Hennage keeps an old-fashioned reaper and binder for use in one of his fields that lies alongside the salt marshes. The field is very wet and soft, so that a combine harvester cannot work without getting bogged down. This retention of the reaper and binder is favorably commented on in the village, not because of the feeling for the land that such an action might imply in another area (see, for example, George Ewart Evans' *Ask the Fellows Who Cut the Hay,* which is concerned with the past agricultural tradition in a village in East Suffolk) but out of admiration for the competence of a farmer who knows his land well and uses that knowledge to get the best return from his land.

ART FORMS: CONCLUSION

The major art forms of Hennage are centered on building, carpentry, and machine design and no longer on agricultural skills, reflecting the present work of core-group members. Art forms are always tied to current expressions of competence, though appreciation of these forms is rooted in the traditions of the past. Art forms are appreciated in terms of design and performance, and the essential of such an appreciation lies in the skills demonstrated in both the construction and use of such items. For the men of the core group their work, which uses and demonstrates their skills and competence to the other members of the group, has the same ritual function that social relationships have for the women. A man's competence is primarily expressed through his work and secondarily through his social relationships. A woman's competence is primarily demonstrated through her skill at social relationships and secondarily through her competence in the house and with the children, although the two fields are, of course, interdependent. Both men and women need membership of the group through links of genealogy or affinity for their competence to have any meaning for their relationships within the group. Hennage people see the demonstration of skills within a work situation, especially a craft occupation, as an art form.

Competences that have little current meaning for the group as expressions of ritual value are little practiced in Hennage by core-group members. Such, for example, is the case with music. I cannot say much about music in Hennage, since very little music is either produced or listened to by core-group members. Possibly music was more important in the past, but on examination it appears that it was enjoyed not on a group basis but on an individual one. I have never heard anyone in Hennage sing, however casually, either to himself or to an audience. Two of the builder's men who worked on our house whistled as they worked—one extremely well—and this was the only music I ever heard produced in Hennage with the exception of Brian Hoveringham and his violin. (Elizabeth Euston has never played the organ in Hennage church, but always those in neighbouring villages; this results from a quarrel between her mother and the Vicar at the date when Elizabeth was learning to play when she was ten.) Roger Crowe has told me that when he was a young man, a number of men in the village played instruments. Most of them belonged to the Methodist Chapel, and on Sunday evenings they would be taken round on a cart to neighboring villages to play hymns and sacred music. Music within a group situation, such as that necessary for church services or village dances, has always been produced by someone outside the core group. Female relations of the current Vicar provide the music for church services, and it was Miss Owens who played the piano for the dances in the Vicarage Rooms. For the dance after the fête I organized, a band was hired from a coastal village, recommended by a villager who had come from there a few years before. No core-group member knew of a band.

Whatever music is heard in Hennage is by courtesy of the popular music programs on the radio, but they are not often listened to. Richard Stevens is apparently unable to work on his car without the aid of pop music, but he is the only one I have noticed regularly to have the radio on for music. Few members of the core group have record players and records, and Brian Hoveringham is the only one to have records of classical music; most core-group members say they "can't stand that row." Music seems to be an expression of individual taste among members of the core group and to have little meaning in the group situation. The dislike of classical music is prevalent throughout the core group and is linked by members to their equal dislike of Art and Drama, which seem to them to belong to an alien tradition and to be part of the world of "Them," and therefore irrelevant to the life of the village.

THE RITUAL OF WORK

As for oral traditions within the core group, all stories I have heard have been directly relevant to the discussion of myth, for all stories had social significance. For this reason they were remembered and retold. The only story I have not recounted does not belong to the core-group members but is an episode involving Lord Stamford, the local builder Roger Crowe, and two of his workmen. The workmen live in Sett, but as the story not only illustrates the relationship between landowner and independent craftsmen but also the ritual nature of skilled craft work, it has some relevance. The workmen were engaged in mending a barn roof at Lord Stamford's residence. It was a tricky job and they had just reached a crucial stage in the work when Lord Stamford appeared and told them to leave it at once to rehang a gatepost that was annoying him. The workmen explained that they had reached a very delicate stage in the repair of the roof and that it would be difficult for them to leave their work just at that moment. Lord Stamford did not accept this answer and shouted up, "If I tell you to come down, you bloody come down. I'm employing you, aren't I?" At this point the workmen came down, and the senior of the two told Lord Stamford that he was not employing them any longer. They then went back to the workshop in Hennage and told Roger Crowe what had happened. That afternoon Mr. Crowe went to Lord Stamford and apologized, but told him that he should not have interrupted the workmen on a job, and even more important, that he should not have sworn at them.

STORYTELLING AND THE PUB

There are few riddles or jokes that people ask each other, and they do not seem to indulge in teasing, but this may be that I have not heard them. The stories I have recounted were all told to me in a one-to-one relationship. I have never been included in a group of people telling stories, although it is possible that such groups may occur in a casual manner. They do not occur in a formalized situation, however. One might think that the public house in the village, the "Black Boys," could have been the center for the social life of the men of the village, but whenever I entered it all conversation stopped until I left. There were rarely more than three or four people in the pub, and not all were necessarily core-group members. There was little of a club atmosphere in the Black Boys; there were no games available, with the exception of darts, and bowls in the summer, no television, and rarely a fire. The brewery company closed it in a rationalization of outlets for their products as it had so little custom.

CHILDREN'S GAMES

Children have their own social life, though now there are not enough of them in a continuing sequence to ensure the maintenance of all traditional pastimes. However, my eldest son, who has been to four primary schools, two in North Norfolk and two in Cambridge, tells me that they played more games and did more traditional things in the local school for Hennage than in any of the other schools he attended. Core-group children used many skipping and ball-game rhymes, as well as counting-out rhymes. The girls played cat's cradle and the boys played conkers.[1] There was a tradition in the village of Valentining, which was performed by the children on St. Valentine's Day. All the children of the village collected together and went round the village in a body to the "big" houses and to houses where they thought they would be given something. When they reached a suitable house, they recited this jingle:

> Good old mother Valentine;
> God bless the . . . [trade of the person who lived in the house]
> God bless the baker.
> You'll be giver
> I'll be taker,
> Good old mother Valentine.

They then banged on the door and the people would come out and give them pennies, oranges, or buns. One old man, the former publican—it is curious that all publicans have been disliked in the village and they are always said to have been disagreeable—was renowned for getting his pennies very hot on a shovel in the fire and then throwing them at the children. This was regarded as low. Valentining

---

[1] Conkers: A series of games played with horse chestnuts suspended on a string. The two players take alternate hits at their opponent's conker with their conker; the player whose conker breaks first loses the game. There are many local variations in naming and scoring.

was still carried on up to the beginning of World War II, and members of the core group that I asked about it think the tradition lapsed for lack of children of the right age.

TRANSMISSION OF APPRECIATION

Just as the sanctions of the core group are diffuse, so too are the means of transmitting the skills and competences approved of by the core group, and of which an appreciation of these skills as art forms is part. All the mechanisms for maintaining the group as a group—norms, attitudes and values, and the sanctions invoked against those who contravene the norms—are diffuse. This diffuseness corresponds to the diffuse nature of the units that construct and appreciate the art forms, or skills, of the group. These units are often made up of two individuals, rarely more than four or five, and are of two different types. The first unit is composed of mature adults and the second mature adults and children. (There is a third type, composed of children, but as I know nothing of what children say to each other in the village, I shall not discuss it.) It is through these small gatherings of individual core-group members that art forms are defined and standards of competence confirmed. The second type of unit, made up of adults and children, or full members of the core group and potential members, divides again into two types. First is the home situation, where the interaction is between parents and children, and second, situations outside the home, where the child is often in the position of hanger-on to a group of adults. The two are not incompatible and may overlap on occasions. For example, Tuesday Clare, one of Desmond Clare's daughters, mentioned that her father would often take some of the children to Blickling Hall, a noted Jacobean mansion near Aylsham, which now belongs to the National Trust. He would show them the house and try to communicate to them his particular passion for the furniture and examples of the art of cabinet-making. When people go out in Hennage it is as a family group, so that at any event, such as the Worstead Festival or the Royal Norfolk Show, there are always children standing by, learning from their elders about the skills and crafts on exhibit and what art forms are significant. The appreciation and knowledge they gain becomes part of them. This educative process is carried on within the home as well, especially for the girls, who learn to clean, sew and knit, and cook at home from their mothers and grandmothers. They also learn the value of competence, not only for the sake of the personal satisfaction for the individual but also for its use in evaluating the competence of others in the group. It is at home or in the village that children, particularly girls, learn the meaning of the ritual of social interaction and the mechanisms or processes of social approval or disapproval. Maybe it is because education in these terms is realistic and satisfying to the girls of the core group that they are so reluctant to go to the school that the educational system imposes on them. Boys have a wider educative field, including garages and workshops, as well as more life on their own. They are more closely linked to the outside world through work, the processes of getting a job and keeping it, and the dependence of local work opportunities on the larger economic system and can therefore see some meaning in attending school.

ART FROM THE OUTSIDE

To Hennage people, education means education for competence, and preferably competence within village terms. It is in the discrepancy between the village competence and the school concept of competence that the conflict between school and village appears. This discrepancy is greatest and the conflict most intense between the village and the grammar school, as illustrated in the histories of the four village children who attended the grammar school. Core-group members recognize that there is a discrepancy between education in their terms and education in a grammar school sense, and they see this discrepancy in terms of work opportunities. In the survey on village attitudes to education mentioned in the Introduction, many parents said, in effect, that they would not mind their children going to grammar school if they thought the children would be able to find work suitable to their capabilities in the neighborhood and if they thought the school would not take their children away from them. This idea is not as far fetched as it sounds. The Norfolk County Education Authority runs a boarding grammar school for which selection is made at the time of the 11+, and the school has a high academic standing. No village children have gone there, but parents usually know of someone whose child has gone, and the impression the parents get is that the children are encouraged to "become middle class" and to leave their own social background. The villagers are unclear whether this should be regarded as right or wrong for the child, and there are arguments on both sides. The villagers would like their children to "have a good job," but not at the expense of having their children cut themselves off. On the other hand, if a child is brilliant, should he not be encouraged to leave a group in which he will be unable to express his brilliance? As I have mentioned, this dilemma has never arisen in its most acute form for a Hennage parent, but it may. The example of Brian Hoveringham, who because he did well at grammar school was able to fill a suitable post in the neighborhood and continue to live in the village, may help. But it seems certain that far more work opportunities that are dependent on academic skills will need to be created before the dilemma is resolved. It is unlikely that this will happen, so the traditional system of the overcompetent and the undercompetent being forced out of the village system, either physically or socially, will continue.

The village appreciation of art forms does not only revolve around the traditional fields of craft skills. Through radio and television villagers are part of the wider society and are capable of being consumers of art and education through these media. In fact, core-group members limit themselves quite drastically out of the media available to them for information and gratification. Everybody who has television, and that means practically everyone, watches Anglia and never the national channels. Radio is little used now, except by those few who do not have television; otherwise it is only used for casual popular music or news. Anglia television is very regional in attitude and program content, with a high proportion of local news and comment. These are the most popular programs in the village, and it is through these local news programs that attitudes and values may be challenged or corroborated. I mentioned earlier that the idea of increased parent participation in the local school had been instigated by the news reports on schools in the area that had experimented with this idea. Anglia also presents a dramatic series with a topical East Anglian theme. Last winter it was called "The New-comers" and centered around the problems of a London working-class family who came to live in an East Anglian village. The series was very popular in Hennage, mainly because the actors had great difficulty with the accent and sounded very funny to local ears. Many of the news items and discussions are around facets of former East Anglian life—the great sailing barges of the east coast, the Yarmouth herring fleet, or Fenland stories, for example. When a book about East Anglian life is published, the author is often interviewed and the book reviewed. Villagers also enjoy the wildlife programs for which Anglia television is famous. There are in the area a number of bird and wildlife reserves, especially on the coast, and as a result of such programs, a surprising number of Hennage people have gone to Blakeney Point to see the terns. A man in the next village, who is a well-known expert on Norfolk dialect, is also an authority on wildlife and has a regular program, which is very popular. Whether this popularity reflects a genuine interest in wildlife or simply local pride is difficult to tell; it could be either or both, as villagers seem to see the program as Norfolk influencing the outside world. As the programs frequently take up the problem of agricultural pollution, the villagers see this as getting at the anonymous "Them" who impose the conditions under which wildlife has to live. A wildlife park and breeding center about twelve miles from Hennage is popular for outings, and the owner frequently appears on Anglia television giving news of the animals.

It is strange that, for all their apparent appreciation of wildlife, very few members of the core group keep animals or household pets; there are a few watch or guard dogs, a couple of budgerigars,[2] and some cats. The cats are necessary because in the winter the rats and mice in the corn fields have a strong inclination to take up residence in the cottages. The men who had allotments and kept pigs between the wars did not seem to remember their pigs with much affection, yet in East Anglia in general, pigs are very highly regarded, as illustrated by the following quotations, the first from an article in the *Eastern Daily Press* and the second from *Akenfield* (Blythe, 1969): "Cats look down on yer, dogs look up at yer, but pigs is equals" and "Pigs is nice sort of people." This latter is especially significant, as animals are usually regarded as "things" in East Anglia.

Finally, the magazines that are read in Hennage are all concerned with skills. Members of the core group take *Amateur Gardener*, *Practical Handiman*, *Mother & Child*, *Woman*, and a few other similar magazines. They all take both local weekly newspapers, which are full of accounts of local weddings and funerals, notices of sales and events, and reports of council meetings, markets, and football matches. Most of the villagers have at some time or another lived in other villages and so know personally or have knowledge of the villages and people whose activities are chronicled in these papers.

I have tried to show that in Hennage art forms are skills and that they reflect the different spheres of competence for men and women. The transmission of these

---

[2] Budgerigars: Small parakeets from Australia, the most popular cage birds in England.

skills and competences is diffuse and takes place either within the home or within a larger social setting, but still within a familiar group. Core-group members see these art forms as being rooted in the past and changed by technological advances or economic necessity imposed on them by the outside world. They use the national media of radio, television, and newspapers very much in regional terms, only selecting items that reinforce their own preferences. It is as if members of the core group are prepared to play a part within the region covered by their own social structure but not to venture outside it. Similarly, they partake only in those art forms which they regard as consistent with their "place" in the local hierarchy; for example, they never go to concerts, although there are many opportunities for this type of recreation, especially in the summer months.

6 / Incomers and outgoers

HENNAGE IN THE WIDER SETTING

So far I have concentrated almost exclusively on members of the core group and their relationships with each other as well as with nonmembers. I may have given the impression by implication that the majority of the ongoing core group remain in the village. This is not so, and indeed it cannot be so, as the village has declined in numbers and most couples—at least in the past—had more than two children. Many potential core-group members have left, but for where and why are problematic. Many are still in the neighborhood, judging by the prevalence of local surnames in nearby villages, a fact which illustrates the thesis that Hennage is part of a wider system of rural proletariat villages. Some leave completely, mostly without trace. For while a few have kept and still keep up their connection with Hennage, far more have not, and the only record of them is the record of their baptism and sometimes a few years on the electoral roll. It must be remembered that for a rural proletariat both jobs and houses are necessary to remaining in the village, so that movement in and out of the village is in part governed by these factors. It is interesting to note that there is a high incidence of marriages between members of the core group and members of similar villages and very few marriages between Hennage people and members of villages where peasant ownership[1] is relatively common. Thus the system of affinal assimilation into another core group widens each member's network for finding housing and work. Affinal assimilation seems to be the normal method of recruitment for the core group, and endogamous marriage, not always demographically impossible, is rare. However, the process of circling through neighboring villages cannot continue indefinitely, and many people leave the district entirely.

PATTERNS OF RESIDENCE AND EFFECTS ON MEMBERSHIP

It seems relevant to ask, "Why these particular people at this particular time?" The reason that the existing core-group members give for the departure of potential members is always in terms of the lack of work and housing, but it must be assumed

---

[1] Peasant ownership: The owning of land, usually in small, fragmented units, by those who work such land.

that some found village life irksome and restrictive. Gregory Dobson was very un-
willing to return after he had spent eleven years as a butcher in a southern town,
and he returned only at the insistence of his wife, who felt that she ought to look
after her widower father. (This is one of the rare endogamous marriages,[2] one of
only two in recent years.) About not wanting to return he says, "There
was too much forelock touching in those days, a man couldn't be his own master."
He is now in his eighties and was referring to the early 1930s. He is also the only
person who does not take the *Eastern Daily Press* among the core group, taking
the *Daily Mirror* instead. There is no evidence at all, however, that it was only
the intelligent and ambitious who left and the dull who remained.

Harold Church remained, and he was a skilled metal-worker. As will be
remembered, he invented a combined vernier scale and slide rule which he cali-
brated in his own units, so that it not only suited his personal tastes but made it
difficult for anyone else to borrow. He first had a job in a workshop at Burgh
railway works, and when the works closed in an engineering workshop in Norwich.
But even if skilled work had not been available at the works in Burgh at this
time, he could have obtained similar work at a blacksmith's, or later at an agricultural machine workshop or garage, given the desire to remain in Hennage. The
other necessity of a house was facilitated for him by the fact that his mother's
family own, as a family, a row of cottages, one of which he has lived in for most
of his married life. He could have obtained a job almost anywhere (according
to himself) but chose to remain in Hennage, and in this he remained faithful to
core-group norms. He followed the same pattern in his working life, for he refused promotion to foreman, remaining as a skilled workman until his retirement.
(This latter information came from the late Thomas Euston, who worked in the
same engineering concern.)

Gregory Dobson is the only person I know of who really wanted to leave the
village system entirely, although it seems likely that the majority who wished to do
so left never to return. I am uncertain as to how general a feeling this was, although the usual reason given by those who stayed for those who left is that there
was not enough work or housing. It does not seem probable that those who left to
live in another similar village disliked the system as such, but very likely moved
because of a lack of housing or employment. The question of housing is important
to the villagers, and there has been a continuous movement from house to house
within the village, although this has slowed down considerably as the number of
owner-occupiers has increased (thanks largely to Miss Owens). There seems to
be no structural reason for moving except that given the size of the cottages, any
chance of moving into a slightly larger one is eagerly taken. The smallest cottages
are at the moment occupied by the newly married or the elderly.

The lack of social mobility among core-group members raises a problem which
I alluded to in the discussion of education in the preceding chapter. The villagers
are aware of this limitation, and the only case I know of where the dilemma had
to be resolved was that of Desmond Clare. He was trained as a carpenter, but
during the time I was in Hennage had risen to the position of clerk of works to

---

[2] Endogamous marriage: A marriage made within the group of which one is a member, as
opposed to exogamous.

the Regional Hospital Board. This was clearly incompatible with core-group norms and he left the village. There was no physical reason why he should have moved; his large family was beginning to disperse, and as he only moved to Burgh, ease of transport can hardly have been the motive. His son, to whom I regularly gave lifts, told me that "Dad couldn't stand living in Hennage any longer; he felt he had to get out." It would seem that the reason Mr. Clare left was that he had become too competent, thus isolating himself from the core group, for he had gone "too far."

Traditionally, the road to social advancement lay through "dealing," as shown by the following quotation, which is taken from C. S. Read: "Recent Improvements in Norfolk Farming," *Journal of the Royal Agricultural Society, 1858:*

> He is a sharp lad, perhaps he keeps rabbits or poultry; he gets a little money together and he buys a pig and afterwards, perhaps, he may start a pony-cart.[3] Then he becomes what we may call a pig-jobber,[4] then perhaps his wife will keep a shop. They might kill a pig in a week and retail it out. Then he would perhaps buy a few sheep and then possibly cattle, and then he would want a bit of land, and then he would go on from one field to another. I could put my hand on dozens of men, I might say, that come on Norwich Hill who have risen in this way to be large farmers or great cattle-dealers, but at the same time, I couldn't put my hand on half-a-dozen men who had risen simply by farming a piece of land.

I asked various members of the core group whether they knew any examples of this type of advancement in Hennage. According to them, and to the registers, there have been only two men who have done this in the last hundred years in Hennage: both came from outside the village, and neither contracted any alliances other than fleeting ones with members of the core group. This demonstrates that it is possible to rise within the parish, although no core-group member has apparently ever done so. It may be the "dealing" which is disliked by the core group, for members openly say, and show, that they dislike "dealers." The only person who ever went to Aylsham market to deal in rabbits, his own and other people's, was Charlie Nobes, who came from outside and was ineffective as a core-group member. The only persons I know of who might well have succeeded in rising in the social scale in this traditional manner are Alfred, Fred, and Florence Clare-Hoveringham and Thomas Lee. They live from their small-holding, which is some of the small percentage of land not owned by Lord Stamford, plus fifteen acres which they rent. However, they do not deal and "get by" quite comfortably, according to themselves, showing no inclination to do better.

THE OUTGOERS

Outgoers thus fall into two categories: those who leave the entire system and those who remain in the system but merely leave Hennage. Almost every member of the core group has at some time or another come into this last category; the only

---

[3] Pony-cart: Having got his pony cart he would become a small-time carrier.

[4] Pig-jobber: One who rears, butchers, sells, and buys pigs.

exceptions are those still too recently married to have done so. I can give no adequate account of the outgoers who leave the system; they are no longer relevant and it is impossible to get information about them. Their relatives who remain seem neither to know nor to care what happens to them except in a few instances where there is personal affection. These last seem to be a third category of outgoers. They leave the system, often for a specific job, but hope to return some day. The Clare relatives who live in Bristol seem to belong to this category, but they are rare. For temporary outgoers, it is more satisfactory to consider their replacements, the incomers.

THE INCOMERS

The incomers form no social group in the village, and they are simply an aggregation of heterogeneous individuals and families who happen to live in Hennage. A single person can, by marriage, become part of the core group, but a married couple can, at best, become honorary members, particularly when their children marry into the core group. But this takes time, and most incomers have already existing ties of genealogy and affinity with other villages; they are expatriate members of other core groups, as are Hennage people when they reside in other villages. Like the outgoers, they can be divided into two categories—those who have lost or abandoned their ties with their place of origin and those who are temporary residents. There is no clear distinction between these groups, however, and with time the boundary becomes blurred. In the first category are all the real outsiders, like the Huntleys, who came from Scotland in the thirties. Even though their daughter was born in Hennage and married a member of a "real Hennage family," they are not themselves accepted as core-group members. Their ties with other people are on a personal level and their acceptance of group norms, though appreciated, does not affect their position. They are the only incomers who come from so far away, except for members of the middle class; the majority of the others come from Norfolk, some from close by, yet neither are these assimilated into the core group. An extreme example of this is the Bugg family, which has been associated with the village since at least the 1820s while its members still maintain their real ties with Castleford. None has ever married a "real Hennage person." Old Austin Bugg had lived most of his life in the village, having been at various times a foundry-man and brazier,[5] postmaster, and tenant farmer at Town Farm; both his sons lived in the village and worked for their father. In spite of the fact that two generations have spent the majority of their lives in Hennage, they are always referred to as "Castleford people"; residence alone is not enough—there must be the genealogical qualification as well. Mr. and Mrs. Shreeve arrived from Massingham about six years ago with two nearly adult children.

---

[5] Brazier: One who works in brass, making household furniture such as bedsteads and fire irons and agricultural trimmings such as horse brasses.

The men work locally, Mr. Shreeve at the garage and his son at Hall Farm; they adhere closely to village norms of behavior; Mrs. Shreeve is a close friend and neighbor of Joan Thurlow—one of the few cases where a nonrelation frequently goes into another's house—and "old lady" Shreeve was already resident in the village. For all their apparent closeness, all the Shreeves are labeled "real Massingham people," and if and when they return to Massingham they will slot neatly back into their own core group. Hennage people living away from the village are in a similar position. This is seen by the ease with which Gregory Dobson was accepted back, although he had intended to stay away for good. Edward Ives, too, is an example of a potential core-group member. He was not born in the village, but his parents were "real Hennage people" who had kept up their ties with the last member of the family resident in the village, Edward's great aunt. She died shortly before he married Beryl Huntley and came to live in a council house in the village. Three years later when I was working on the lists of "real Hennage people" he was on every core-group member's list and on many of the others as well.

In no sense do the incomers form a group. Two incoming families living close together may become friendly, but it depends on personality. The Shreeves and the Marshes both come from Massingham, live opposite one another, and have members of their family working on Hall Farm, but have no other relationship. They say "hello" and chat a bit, but they do not visit each other or appear more friendly than with anyone else. They do not form a clique, nor are they thought of by "real Hennage people" as doing so. Although both families are known to come from Massingham, they are never referred to as a unit "that Massingham lot" but as the individual families. Similarly, the incomers are never regarded by the core group as a group, not even as "those who are not Hennage people." When one asks questions about them, they are always placed in reference to their known or believed village of origin, or to the village they last lived in.

On the whole, the incomers fit in very well. They accept and conform to core-group norms, and relationships with them seem to be based on the closeness of their conformity. But these relationships are only in individual terms, and the incomers form no group. The only occasions on which the core group is hostile toward incomers is over the question of the allocation of council houses,[6] since members tend to feel that council houses in Hennage should be for "real Hennage people." The hostility is not directed toward the incomers but against the authorities who make the allocations, as is shown by the rapid acceptance of the individual incomers concerned. The Williams were resented at first, yet are now on perfectly good terms with the core group; Norman and Barbara Taylor were similarly resented but soon settled in; and the Yallops were disliked initially for taking over a council

---

[6] Allocation of council houses: Since the council houses are owned and managed by each local council, a family wishing for such subsidized housing applies to the local Council and is placed on the list. Where they are placed is determined by the degree of need and urgency. Those rising to the top of the list are allocated the first available council house, irrespective of their place of origin within the area covered by the local Council and irrespective of the time spent on the list.

house coveted and expected by a "proper Hennage couple," but the dislike on this account soon faded, to be replaced by dislike of them as individuals. The resentment continues in everyday conversation, but it is clearly directed at "Them," the authorities, for not paying attention to the needs of "real Hennage people."

7 / Conclusions

Up until now I have made no reference to other studies of English village life. This is largely because there is not a lot of literature on the subject and what there is is of a very different nature. It is curious that nearly all studies have been made in the west of England and that in every case the pattern of landholding has been totally different. They are not studies of rural proletariats. Williams (1956, 1963) is concerned with communities of small farmers owning their own land. In the former study the main interest is in the way Cumberland farmers interact and the functions they perform; in the latter he analyzes the way in which Devon farmers change their holdings and looks at the rise and fall of farming families. In neither does the base of the social system receive systematic treatment, for Williams is not concerned with these people. Similarly, Little-john (1963) in his study of a Scottish border village is concerned with the way the total village fits into the larger economic sphere rather than in the relationships between villagers. Here again the major social figures are small independent farm-ers. Frankenberg (1957) in his study of a Welsh border village emphasizes "Religion, Politics and Football" in his search for the leaders of the community. All of these studies have been in Celtic or Celtic fringe areas and seem very different in historical background and culture; this, taken in connection with the total variance of landholding patterns, makes fruitful comparison tricky. If I had concentrated on the relationship between gentry and landowner it might have been possible, but it was specifically the internal relationships within the core group which interested me, and this is scarcely considered in the other works.

The only detailed studies I know of which are concerned with East Anglian village life are nonanthropological. George Ewart Evans has written four books on the past life of two Suffolk villages, in which he is mainly involved with the validity of oral tradition and the unbroken continuity of many farming methods. They are wholly fascinating books, but the structural nature of the villages is im-plicit and can only be extracted piecemeal, and there are, from my point of view, several lacunae. Further, Evans is interested in the past, and he is dealing with reminiscences with little mention of what is happening now. This is not to cast aspersions on his work; we are simply interested in different problems. I think it is sufficient to say that there is little in his books which runs counter to my findings; we are both working on areas within the same social system. The other writer who has recently concerned himself with East Anglian life is Ronald Blythe, who collected information on the past in *Akenfield*, again in Suffolk. On reading this book I found that many details and attitudes among Akenfield people are the same as in Hennage, but Blythe makes no attempt to analyze these; he is a writer not an anthropologist. In particular, the relationship between the "big house" and the village is illuminating, although in Akenfield the landowner is resident in the village. It is only in points of great detail that differences between Akenfield and Hennage seem to arise; there are no major contradictions. Incidentally, the heavy sales of all these books in East Anglia affirms the awareness of a regional identity.

Throughout this study I have attempted to see the total social situation from the viewpoint of a core-group member, although the analysis is, of course, done from an observer's position. The total social situation is one rooted in the past—a past when the power of the landowner was more real than it is now. Everything still revolves round this attitude, and the identity of the village community is seen in these terms. This is partly due to the Vicar's nonfulfillment of his role, but other aspects of core-group life constantly reaffirm it—their concept of "place," their ritual life, and the nature of their own, as opposed to the official, educational process. Having spent much time in identifying the core group, I should perhaps emphasize that the majority of noncore-group villagers also adhere to core-group norms. They have largely the same concept of "place," their attitudes toward the social hierarchy are basically the same as those of the core group, and their children, while they remain in the village, mix with other children and are subject to more or less the same social conditioning. The measure of this similarity is seen in the difficulty I had in identifying the core group and that in the educational attitude survey I got no hint from the findings that the villagers are not homogeneous. This is a similarity which would seem to stem from the fact that most incomers arrive from villages of broadly similar standing in the social system and would be, if they had stayed in their natal villages, members of their own core group. The reciprocal nature of the concept of "place" reaffirms for all the continued existence of the total social system, and the concept of "competence" and the diffuse nature of the mechanisms that maintain social cohesion serve to confirm their own "place" in the hierarchy. The diffuse nature of the educational process and the reinforcement of social sanctions necessitate equally diffuse mechanisms of change. The landowner to some extent takes part in this. The pattern of landowning has not changed, and although there have been new administrative institutions, these are filled with the same people who formerly performed the traditional administrative functions. The nature of the men's work has changed in part, though crafts were always important, but the social values and ritual involved in this have changed their expression rather than the basic values, which appear to have remained unaltered. Everything thus conspires to confirm the nature of the hierarchy. As the landholding has not changed and the dependence on the landowner has only recently diminished, it is hardly surprising that the attitudes and social values of the core group should still continue. That they do continue is clear, and this continuity is tacitly accepted by both ends of the scale, though probably only partially in the case of the landowner. The chain—from landowner to gentry to villager—is seen to the exclusion of the wider political and economic fields, which seem so remote as to be irrelevant. As far as the villagers are concerned, it is a "Them and Us" situation; "They" control the outside, "We" only control our own social life, which assumes magnified importance; it is all that is left. Thus social relationships are largely intragroup; intergroup relationships are conducted through a mediator and apart from the circumscribed contact, which is hardly active at the moment, the groups at the base tend to live in isolation.

In fairness to the reader it must be pointed out that the facts I have observed must inevitably have been conditioned by my major interest in the continuity and cohesion of the village as a community. Had I been interested particularly in change, I might have noticed more factors pointing in this direction. I have been aware of this possible bias throughout and, in my own defense, must stress that the evidence for change which I have found has all been presented in this study. Change does not appear to come from within the group *qua* group, but involves a slight alteration of emphasis in norms, a change only noticeable over a longer period of years than I have been resident in Hennage. Change can be seen as a readjustment of norms by the group in response to changing conditions imposed on them by the outside world.

Finally, I feel that the true framework for comparative analysis of this material would be in terms of other systems organized around "Them" and "Us" situations.

Recommended Reading

BRITISH RURAL STUDIES

Frankenberg, R., *Village on the Border: A Study of Religion, Politics and Football in a North Wales Community*. London, Cohen and West, 1957.

Frankenberg, R., *Communities in Britain*. London, Harmondsworth, 1966.
  A good short survey usefully summarizing a variety of community studies. The theoretical considerations seem to be obscure and do not appear to tie in very closely with modern anthropological theory.

Littlejohn, J., *Westrigg: A Cheviot Parish*. London, International Library of Sociology and Social Reconstruction, 1963.
  I found this to have little direct relevance, but others might find it useful in considering change in a rural community.

Williams, W. M., *The Sociology of an English Village: Gosforth*. London, International Library of Sociology and Social Reconstruction, 1956.

Williams, W. M., *A West Country Village: Ashworthy*. London, Dartington Hall Studies in Rural Sociology, 1963.
  Both books deal largely with the relationships among farmers, landowners, and gentry. The base of the hierarchy is hardly considered in structural terms. Sociological rather than anthropological.

All of these studies, except for urban studies in communities in Britain, are concerned with Celtic and Celtic-fringe communities, and the patterns of landholding are very different from those in Hennage. They are not concerned with rural proletariats and are therefore of limited use for comparative purposes. They also have their own interest, however.

OTHER EAST ANGLIAN STUDIES

Blythe. R., *Akenfield*. New York: Dell Publishing Company, 1969.

Evans, G. E., *Ask the Fellows Who Cut the Hay*. London, Faber, 1956.

Evans, G. E., *The Horse in the Furrow*. London, Faber, 1960.

Evans, G. E., *The Pattern under the Plough*. London, Faber, 1967.

Evans, G. E., *Where Beards Wag All*. London, Faber, 1970.

These books are all fascinating and among them give a very clear picture of the continuity in agricultural and social tradition in East Anglia. They are particularly concerned with the validity of oral tradition and therefore scarcely consider structural implications. For the flavor of past rural life they are highly recommended.

OTHER EUROPEAN STUDIES

Barnes, J., "Class and Committees in a Norwegian Parish," *Human Relations* 7, 1954, 39–58.
Morin, E., *Plodémet*. London, Penguin Press, 1971.
Pitt-Rivers, J., *The People of the Sierra*, 2d ed. Chicago, University of Chicago Press, 1971.

"THEM" AND "US"

Barth, F., *Nomads of South Persia: The Basseri Tribe of the Khumesh Confederacy.* Oslo, Oslo University Press, 1961.
Barth, F., (ed.), *Ethnic Groups and Boundaries*. Boston, Little, Brown, 1969.
Campbell, J. K., *Honour, Family and Patronage: The Sarakatsani*. Oxford, Oxford University Press, 1964.
Colson, E., *The Makah Indians*. Manchester, England, Manchester University Press, 1953.
Turnbull, C., *The Forest People*. New York, Simon & Schuster, 1968.
Turnbull, C., *The Wayward Servants: The Two Worlds of the African Pygmies.* London, Eyre, 1966.

The above are concerned, in some measure, with "them" and "us" situations and throw light on the effects this has on the value systems of the people involved.

THEORY

Gluckman, M., and E. Devons, *Closed Systems and Open Minds: The Limits of Naivety in Social Anthropology.* Edinburgh, University of Edinburgh Press, 1964.

A salutary reminder that one's knowledge is limited and a useful guide to how far one may rely on one's common sense.

Leach, E., *Political Systems of Highland Burma*. London, London School of Economics, 1954.
Radcliffe-Brown, A. R., *Structure and Function in Primitive Society*. London, Cohen and West, 1952.